DRONACHARYA
AT THE WORKPLACE
➤—— AND OTHER SHORT STORIES ——➤

MEGHDOOT KARNIK

First Printing, 2016
Printed in India

ISBN: 978-93-83952-86-1

Editing: Roona Ballachanda, Wordit CDE
Cover Design: Wordit CDE

The Write Place
A Publishing Initiative by Crossord Bookstores Ltd.
Paradigm, A-Wing, 1st Floor, Mindspace, Link Road,
Malad West, Mumbai 400064, India.

Web: www.TheWritePlace.in
Facebook: TheWritePlace.in
Twitter: @WritePlacePub
Instagram: @WritePlacePub

Printed At: Parksons Graphics, Mumbai

ACKNOWLEDGEMENTS

I never set out to be a writer. Around fifteen years ago, a friend enrolled me to write a textbook on accounting. I wrote it in my own style which promptly got rejected. Till the end of 2014, I had never thought in my wildest dreams, that I would write a book.

I am a huge believer in destiny. Over the last few years, I have been fatalistic. Not that I have surrendered to fate, but have had experiences, which clearly tell me, that howsoever hard you try, if it is not meant to be, it will not be. At the same time, I have had a few surprises, some long standing dreams being fulfilled, out of the blue.

In early 2015, God sent me an Angel. For some reason, I showed her the fifteen year old project. She motivated me to write. Her specific words were "You have a gift, you should write." The seed was planted and it started taking root. I knew nothing about the publishing industry, had no contacts, and did not have any idea how to approach publishers.

One evening, I went to Crossword to buy a gift for the Angel. I saw a placard about The Write Place, offering publishing services. It is eerie that both the writing advice and the publishing opportunity arose from the Angel or events pertaining to her. If it is a coincidence, I think it is an extremely curious coincidence. I connected the two events, recognised the signals and commenced writing. I think this book is a result of planets aligning and elements coming together.

I wrote the first draft of my first story and sent it to her for feedback. She trashed it big time. Her email giving qualitative feedback has gone a long way towards improving my writing skills and the making of this book. Thank you God and thank you dear Angel.

I would like to thank the Wordit CDE team for their support in this entire process, with special mention of my editor Roona Ballachanda. Thanks Roona for your critical eye while going through the manuscript.

This book would never have been possible without my wife Sheetal. Announcing that I am writing a book, when I had never written anything in the fifteen years of our marriage, was reason enough to classify me as a lunatic. Credit goes to her that she supported me and did not consign me to an asylum.

She has been a continuous sounding board for ideas, and has also been subjected to the torture of reading multiple drafts of every story. She has been kind enough to bear my idiosyncratic behaviour. Sheetal, this book is dedicated to you. Thank you for your continuous support, feedback, critical review and most importantly for being there.

CONTENTS

Acknowledgements   3

Introduction   7

Key characters in the Mahabharata   9

Dronacharya at the workplace   15

Recruiting Karna   32

Arjuna's mistake   52

Bhishma's silence   71

Karna's reputation   93

Abhimanyu   115

Yudhishthir's Dilemma   137

Kunti & Karna   151

About the Author   169

INTRODUCTION

It is said, "Take any situation in regular life, and you will find it in the Mahabharata." It is, in a sense a complete epic. While the Mahabharata is supposed to be the triumph of good over evil, every character has its shades of grey. In this book, I have tried to explore how the Mahabharata can be used as a reference point to solve dilemmas in corporate life.

At this point I would like to differentiate between religion and mythology. In India, for a lot of people any reference to the Ramayana and Mahabharata is about its relevance to our culture, our glorious past, our rich heritage etc. At the same time, there are a lot of other people, who look at these epics as just another story. It is not that these people are not religious. They worship their own gods (and there are a whole lot of them in India) but at the same time are open to exploring various interpretations of these epics, without sitting in judgement on them or their characters.

Every action has a reaction which is based on perception. Each action, if looked at from a different prism, can give a different interpretation. This book tries to look at various incidents in the Mahabharata from different perspectives. The interpretation of characters' thoughts is simply an attempt to draw parallels to corporate life and learn from them. While the situations portrayed are based on the reading of the Mahabharata, the perceptions, thoughts and insights are the creative liberty of the author. There is no intention whatsoever to pass a judgement on any of the characters.

The incidents in corporate life are purely a figment of my imagination, created to fit the situations in the Mahabharata. In the journey of writing this book, I discovered how easily the Mahabharata fits into these situations.

I have been advised that not everybody has read the Mahabharata, and people may not necessarily relate to the stories. This book is not about the Mahabharata, and it is impossible to write the story of the epic in a few pages. Even if I attempt the same, I will always be guilty of leaving some or the other important piece out. Hence I am providing a brief introduction to the major characters which appear in the book.

I hope the reader also appreciates the associations at a transactional level and enjoys the reading experience.

KEY CHARACTERS IN THE MAHABHARATA

Simply told, the Mahabharata is a fight over a kingdom between two sets of cousins (Kauravas – 100 sons and 1 daughter) and the Pandavas (5 sons). It results in an epic battle which is won by the Pandavas. As it is a tale of destruction, old-timers do not like to keep a copy of the Mahabharata at home. They prefer to keep the "Bhagvad Gita", a discourse by Krishna to Arjuna when he was hesitant to fight against his own cousins and relatives. The "Bhagvad Gita" is also the holy book of the Hindus.

Profiles of Key Characters from the Mahabharata who appear in this book.

1. **Bhishma** – A father figure to both, the Kauravas and the Pandavas, Bhishma was their paternal grand uncle. Early in his life, he took a wow to stay unmarried, so that his father could remarry and also promised not to stake claim to the throne and to be loyal to the king of the clan of Kuru or the Kauravas.

2. **Pandu** – The father of the Pandavas, Pandu was cursed by a sage that if he ever got intimate with any woman, he would die instantly. The five sons of his two wives (Kunti and Madri) are called the descendants of Pandu or the Pandavas; however he is not the biological father of any of them.

Even though he was the younger brother, he was appointed king, as Dhritarashtra his elder brother was born blind. After the curse, he decided to live life as a hermit with his two wives and handed over the throne to Dhritarashtra. One day in the forest, he could not resist the beauty of Madri, his second wife and died the instant he touched her intimately.

3. **Kunti** – The first wife of Pandu and mother of three of the Pandavas. In her young age, she had served sage Durvasa, who was known for his hot temper. He granted her a boon, that if she invoked any of the gods, they could bear her a child. Before her marriage, she wanted to test if the boon worked and hence invoked the Sun God and Karna was born. Because Karna was born out of wedlock, she abandoned him at birth. Post marriage, she bore three sons, Yudhishthir (son of Yama, the God of Death), Bheema (son of Vayu, the God of Wind) and Arjuna (son of Indra, the King of Gods). After the death of Pandu and Madri, she moved with the five children of Pandu to Hastinapur.

4. **Madri** – The second wife of Pandu. After her three children, Kunti passed on her boon to Madri, who invoked the Ashwini twins (the Gods of medicine) and bore two children Nakul and Sahadev. She could not bear the grief of being the cause of her husband Pandu's death and hence jumped into his funeral pyre.

5. **Dhritarashtra** – The father of the Kauravas who was born blind. Though he was elder to Pandu, Pandu was appointed on the throne as a blind person was deemed

physically incapable to rule. Later when Pandu retired to the forest with his wives, Dhritarashtra became king. This was one of the reasons for the controversy, as to who was the successor to the throne – Duryodhan, the eldest son of Dhritarashtra, or Yudhishtir, the eldest son of Pandu.

6. **Gandhari** – Dhritarashtra's wife, who, after she learnt that her husband was blind, decided to blindfold herself for life.

7. **Yudhishthir** – The eldest of the Pandavas and the son of Yama, the God of Death. He was the epitome of righteousness and hence was also known as 'Dharmaraj', the upholder of right. His sense of Dharma (Call of Duty) prevented him from speaking a lie. Hence he was reputed for always speaking the truth. But, he loved gambling and gambled away his kingdom, his brothers and their wife Draupadi in a game of dice.

8. **Bheema** – The second son in the Pandava lineage and the son of Vayu the Wind God. He was known for his exemplary strength and brawn.

9. **Arjuna** – The third son in the Pandava lineage and the son of Indra, the King of the Gods. He was known to be an archer par excellence and the favourite of Dronacharya, the royal teacher.

10. **Nakul and Sahadev** – The youngest of the Pandavas, twins, and sons of Madri granted as a boon to her by the twin Gods, Ashwini-Kumara.

11. **Duryodhana** – Eldest son of Dhritarashtra and Gandhari and the eldest among 101 children. He

ascended the throne of Hastinapur and his refusal to give even an inch of land to the Pandavas resulted in the final war.

12. **Karna** – The eldest son of Kunti and Surya, the Sun God, he was abandoned at birth and was raised by Adhirath, a charioteer. He was born with Kavacha-Kundala, an armour and gold earrings, which made him invincible. In the prevailing caste system, he was always considered inferior to the princes. He was trained by the sage Parashurama and was as great an archer as Arjuna if not better. He gate crashed the graduation ceremony of the princes' and proceeded to surpass all of Arjuna's achievements. He was not awarded the prize of the best archer, as he was a mere charioteer's son, Duryodhana, on the spot, crowned him a prince and the King of Anga and made him an equal. Thus began a friendship which stood the test of time. He was also known to be 'Daan Veer' an epitome of charity.

13. **Draupadi** – Draupadi was the common wife of the five Pandavas. Arjuna had won her hand by winning the contest, which required the skilled archer to pierce the eye of a wooden fish on a rotating board, by looking at its reflection in the water. When he, along with his brothers reached home, they said, "Look mom what we have got." Kunti said, "Whatever you have, share it equally among all brothers." Thus she ended up getting married to five men. Extremely beautiful, she was gambled away by Yudhishthir in a game of dice which led to an attempt to disrobe her in an open court.

14. **Dronacharya** - Dronacharya was the royal teacher of the 105 princes. His favouritism towards Arjuna was well known. He fought the war on the side of the Kauravas. He employed the deadly Chakravyuh formation in battle on the thirteenth day, which resulted in the death of Abhimanyu. When he was told in the war that his son Ashwatthama was killed, he lost the will to fight and laid down his arms.

15. **Abhimanyu** – Son of Arjuna and Subhadra (one of Arjuna's many wives), he was as great a warrior as his father. He had learnt the technique of breaking the Chakravyuha formation when he was in his mother's womb. Unfortunately Subhadra fell asleep halfway during the narration and hence he did not know how to exit the same and so, was trapped inside during the war.

16. **Krishna** – Krishna was a cousin of the Pandavas and was raised as a cowherd. He was the key person who guided the Pandavas to victory from time to time. He was also the charioteer of Arjuna in the war. On the first day of war, Arjuna was not ready to fight, as he had his brothers, uncles, teachers and other relatives in the opposition. That is when Krishna recited the 'Bhagvad Gita' and convinced Arjuna to fight. He is a reincarnation of Lord Vishnu. All the other characters in the Mahabharata are only recognised as such, while Krishna is revered as a God.

This is by no means an exhaustive list of characters. The Mahabharata by itself is a complex epic, and has multiple tracks and characters running in parallel throughout the narrative.

DRONACHARYA AT THE WORKPLACE

"I shall see you on Tuesday at 9." Twisha didn't reply and hung up the phone. It was Sujoy, her ex-manager who was on the call. He had just offered her a job with a hefty pay increase and a promotion, and she was not sure whether she should take it up.

Twisha was a Senior Associate at Tomfina. Leading a team of 30, she was one of the top talents in the company and earmarked for growth. Intelligent, soft spoken and assertive, she was highly respected by her peers, and both her juniors and seniors had huge faith in her.

She had been thrust into this leadership position two months ago, when Sujoy had quit. Sujoy had been a Vice President and Twisha's manager. Quite a few people including Twisha were upset that Sujoy had quit leaving a huge void in the company. The management was not sure whether Twisha was ready to take over Sujoy's role, but at the same time had confidence in her. They decided against finding a replacement for Sujoy and persisted with Twisha.

In her current role, Twisha was like a bird learning to fly. Sujoy's leaving was like the mother pushing the baby out of the nest. The bird tries to fly, falls down a few times, but eventually learns to fly. Twisha was exactly in that situation. For the first time in her career, she was struggling, learning, getting beaten up... but gaining immensely from the experience.

Another challenge was that people, who were her peers two months ago, were now reporting to her. She had to balance the delicate act of managing "friends" which is extremely tricky. Suddenly, people become wary of the "manager" and don't know how much information to share, and how much to trust this person who was once their equal and friend but now, their manager. Ultimately appraisals are done by the manager and everybody wants to be in the manager's good books.

She was juggling managing her team, managing her stakeholders, both local and international, as well as doing her regular work. The scope of her work had increased manifold and she was discovering herself. At the same time there were days of frustration, where she would curse Sujoy for leaving her in the lurch.

Twisha's tryst with Sujoy began seven years ago, when she joined his team as an analyst. Her hard work, intelligence and analytical abilities had impressed him. In a matter of few months Twisha had become Sujoy's go to person and would get pulled into every high profile project. Sujoy himself was extremely brilliant. Both of them fed off each other. Twisha learnt a lot about the business, analysis and strategic decision making from Sujoy. Sujoy would in turn rely upon Twisha to generate reams of data and make sense of the numbers. Both of them enjoyed working with each other.

Sujoy had moved two organisations and Twisha had followed him. She was getting what she wanted; better pay and working with a great person. What more does one want? Tomfina was the third organisation where Twisha was working with Sujoy.

And now Sujoy had quit. He wanted Twisha to follow him and join him. However, this time Twisha was not so sure.

When Sujoy quit, she was thrust into his role. She was no longer a fresh analyst. By virtue of multiple job changes she was ahead of her peers. The role was tough. After all how can one replace seventeen years of experience with seven? She knew that if she succeeded in doing Sujoy's role well, the Vice President position was not far away.

And here was Sujoy offering her the Vice President position on a platter. With a hefty pay increase, the offer couldn't be better. However, she knew that if she left Tomfina, people would be unhappy. Nobody from her juniors could take up the role and the department would struggle. In her mind she knew that it was not the right thing to do. However the offer was tempting enough and her career would be fast tracked. She decided to pack up and go home and think about it over the weekend. However Twisha couldn't mask her emotions and the turmoil in her mind.

She reached home, threw her bag on the table and sat down to read. Suddenly the roar on the TV from Karan's room irritated her.

Karan was her younger brother. Both of them were as different as chalk and cheese. Twisha was intelligent, sincere, extremely hard working and would study 14 to 16 hours a day and was the quintessential topper. She would get extremely tense and worked up before every exam and also about the results.

Karan on the other hand was bright, intelligent, always close to the top, but never the topper. His interests were varied and he would have long discussions with his friends on various topics. These discussions ranged from cricket, football, RSS, Rahul Gandhi, Narendra Modi, Malala Yousafzai, Obama, the Mahabharata and everything else under the sun. Nobody knew when he studied. Extremely witty and intelligent, he was the Buddha. He had taken a year off and was preparing for CAT.

CAT or the Common Aptitude Test, is the test for entry into the Indian Institutes of Management (IIM) which are prestigious institutes. An entry into an IIM is a confirmed ticket to a successful career.

Twisha thought that if Karan would put in a little bit more effort, he would be a topper. She just did not agree with Karan's methods and thought he was wasting his time.

Karan was in a foul mood today. The events of the day had affected him. A BJP minister had passed a racist comment on the Congress President. Another BJP Chief Minister had made a similarly awful statement, which said that dark women don't easily get grooms.

"Why can't these guys keep their mouths shut? They have a mandate to govern for five years and with every step they raise to put their foot forward, they end up putting it in their mouth. I mean human feet aren't exactly edible."

While he was discussing this issue with his friends, some actually had a view that this was the truth. This angered Karan even more. The icing on the cake was Deepika Padukone. Vogue had just released a video on Women Empowerment with Deepika Padukone. Karan thought this was just brilliant and strong and showed it to his friends.

Their reactions shocked him. Some girls said that the video would corrupt young girls. The guys said that it was a justification for adultery. Karan realised that education isn't everything in life. Mind-sets need to change and maybe it will take generations for any significant changes to happen. He just kept quiet. He came home seething in anger and switched on the music at full blast to crowd out his anger.

Today the conflict in Twisha's mind clashed with the music. And there was an explosion.

"How many times do I have to tell you to reduce the volume? Don't you see I am tired after a full day's work? The least I expect is some peace in the house."

"For peace you need to go to the temple. *Wahaan bhi aarti ke time shanti nahin hoti.*" Karan and his wisecracks.

Now Twisha snapped and started barking at Karan and the two of them had a big showdown. It ended with both of them slamming the doors of their respective rooms and shutting each other out. An irritated Twisha didn't even come out for dinner.

At eleven in the night Karan knocked on Twisha's door.

"Kya chahiye?" (What do you want?)

"Twisha I am sorry. I have shut off the music. Let's have dinner."

"I am not hungry."

"Wow! You survive on love and fresh air!! *Mujhe bhi sikhao na how to do that. Waise mere pet mein bhi chuhe daud rahe hain."(Wonder how you do that. By the way, even I have not eaten and am extremely hungry)*

Brother-sister fights are usually like this. They fight fiercely, but the underlying bond of love always remains intact. Most brothers are hugely protective of their sisters. And sisters are emotional, especially when it comes to their younger brothers. The fact that Karan had not eaten, melted Twisha's heart and she came out. They started eating dinner at the dining table.

"What's your problem sis?" Karan asked.

"What do you mean? I don't have any problems."

"Come on Twisha, I have known you for 23 years now. Your face is an open book"

"You don't know anything about corporate life. How can you help?"

"I am not asking you to narrate the problem so that I can solve it. If you tell me the problem two things will happen. You will feel lighter. Also in the process of retelling, you will actually understand the root cause of the problem. This will only help yourself. But you know I have solutions for Narendra Modi, on how to run this country. The problem is he doesn't listen to me!"

Trust Karan to defuse a tense situation with humour! Twisha now narrated the dilemma she was facing.

"You know Sujoy?"

"Your ex-boss... He has left Tomfina right?"

"He wants me to join him in the new organisation. He is offering me a Vice President post and a hefty pay hike."

"Great Twisha! What else do you need? Now your additional income can finance a new bike for me."

"It is not that easy Karan. I am doing well in my current role. It is a huge responsibility and a time to prove myself. But now, this tempting offer…"

"Temptation is sin."

"You and your stupid one liners!!"

"Ok, let's change the topic. Who do you think was the best archer in the Mahabharata?"

"Arjuna of course."

"Are you sure?"

"What are you hinting at?"

"Let me explain. There is the famous story of the archery test of the Kauravas and Pandavas. One day Guru Dronacharya took the Kauravas and the Pandavas to the forest with their bows and arrows. He had placed a stuffed parrot on a tree far away. The task was to pierce the eye of the parrot. He called them one by one and asked them to take position and aim at the target. Before they could shoot, they were asked to describe what they saw. Dronacharya asked them to focus. One prince said he saw a parrot on the branch of the tree. Dronacharya asked him to step aside. Another said he saw a green parrot. Even he was asked to step aside. One by one they came and described the surroundings along with the parrot and the trees. None of them was allowed to shoot at the target. When it was Arjuna's turn, he said he saw the eye of the parrot. Dronacharya asked him, 'Do you see anything else'. Arjuna said, 'No I see only the eye of the parrot'. Dronacharya then allowed only Arjuna to shoot the arrow."

"Great story Karan. It tells you the importance of focus. I keep on telling you, you waste your time everyday watching movies, listening to music, watching TV etc. God knows when you study! If you want to crack the CAT and get into a great institute, you need to have focus in life."

"Thanks for the sisterly advice Twisha, but I have a different point. Do you realise that out of the 105 kids there, only one was given the opportunity? The rest were side-lined. Do you realise even they were good archers and some of them could actually have hit the parrot's eye?"

"Interesting point Karan, but opportunities knock at the door of only those who are focussed."

"Who gave the opportunity Twisha? Did Arjuna grab it or did Dronacharya give it?"

"There is no difference. What matters is Arjuna was the best archer and he proved it by piercing the parrot's eye."

"Why do you think I am named Karan?"

"What has that got to do with Arjun?"

"Tune suna nahin... Rakhee kehti hain... 'Mere Karan Arjun aayenge'!! Kabhi Hindi picture bhi dekha karo Twisha"

"Aaargh!!!" Twisha let out a sigh in anguish. She was used to Karan's PJs but this was bad by even his standards.

"Bakwaas band kar Karan!!"

"Okay. Answer my question."

"Dad and mom liked the name, simple"

"Who is dad's favourite character from the Mahabharata?"

"Now I get it, it is Karna and hence you were named Karan."

"Do you realise that Karna was as equally skilled as Arjuna? And then there was Eklavya, who had to offer his thumb as a Gurudakshina to Dronacharya"

"I get your point Karan, Arjuna may not have been the best archer, but he was up there. And what is Arjuna's fault in all this?"

"Nothing. Arjuna is not at fault at all. Some people are just lucky."

"Listen Karan, people are lucky because they work hard."

"Ok sorry. No doubt Arjuna worked hard, was very skilled and extremely talented. He was even top of the class. But throughout the Mahabharata, Arjuna was protected. First by Dronacharya and then in the battlefield by Krishna."

"So what? He was successful."

"Yes he was. But had he been left to himself, would he have survived or won the battle?"

"You may be right Karan. But that is where Krishna and Dronacharya have played the role of mentors and teachers."

"Good point Twisha. Remember, at the start of the war, he wanted to lay down his arms, as he did not want to fight his brothers. It is only when Krishna recited the Gita, and told him his 'Dharma', that he agreed to fight the war."

"I think Arjuna was extremely talented to win the war. The conflict over fighting his brothers is natural. If he had laid down the arms, maybe the war wouldn't have happened. Arjuna was just not convinced that it was right to go to war. Also when one is confronted with relatives as adversaries, the decision is all the more difficult. I mean tomorrow, if I have to sack somebody who is related to us, it will be extremely difficult. Forget sacking, if I am interviewing one of our cousins, trust me Karan, the decision will be difficult. While I will still be true to the firm and not compromise on quality, I might subconsciously think of reasons to hire him or her."

Twisha was now enjoying this conversation. She did not know where it was headed, but it was a huge diversion from Sujoy's offer and she began to feel herself relax a bit. Silently, she was thanking Karan for diverting her mind from the demons it faced. The combative spirit in her was determined to beat up every argument from Karan.

"Good Twisha, now we are warming up. It's been long since I have had some interesting discussions with you. Let's discuss this issue in greater detail."

"When Dronacharya, gave only Arjuna the opportunity to fire the arrow, what would the other students have felt?"

"I don't know, you tell me…"

"I am sure they would have felt cheated. I am sure, quite a few of them believed that even they could have hit the parrot's eye. They would have been unhappy at being denied the opportunity. To me this is the first seed of rivalry that eventually led to the war. If you read various narratives of the Mahabharata, Arjuna was clearly Dronacharya's favourite student. This led to Dronacharya spending more time with him and teaching him much more."

"Karan, this happens even in corporate life. The best people are the favourites of managers, and get the most challenging projects. Their development is thus fast tracked and they rise much faster in the organisation."

"But history still debates whether Arjuna is the best archer. There is no unanimity on that. Do you want to be the best archer or Dronacharya's Arjun?"

"What do you mean Karan?"

Karan didn't reply. He had innocuously slipped in a statement, and wanted Twisha to understand the enormity of the same.

It took a few seconds for Twisha to understand the impact of Karan's statement. Now she became serious and in a calm and firm voice asked,

"What exactly are you hinting at Karan?"

Karan realised that Twisha had become serious. The casual conversation started acquiring a serious tone. He was close to hitting a raw nerve and the situation had to be tackled carefully. He discarded the sarcasm and casualness from his voice.

"See, don't get me wrong. Everybody needs a Dronacharya to grow and learn. Nobody comes out learned from the mother's womb. But after a certain point, once you have grown wings, you need to fly on your own strength."

"Interesting point." Twisha was ruminating about Karan's words. The impact was slowly sinking in.

"Let me ask you another question Twisha. Do people in your current organisation think that you are in your current position because of Sujoy?"

Now this was a bit too much for Twisha. The raw nerve which Karan was trying to avoid, twitched. Twisha flew off the handle. "Don't ever say that. I am at my position purely on my talent and hard work. You good for nothing, have not even started corporate life, and have the impudence to talk like this!"

Twisha's anger was evident in her tone. The situation had to be defused.

"If I have offended you Twisha, I am sorry. I completely agree that you are extremely talented and hard working. I am actually very proud of you. But calm down and listen to my question again. Do your colleagues think in this fashion?"

This time Twisha did not reply. Her seven year career flashed across her eyes. She had left her peers behind. The fact that she was Sujoy's favourite was an open secret. There were murmurs that her fast rise was due to Sujoy. However she alone knew how hard she had worked. Sujoy was a hard taskmaster.

Actually for the first six months, she had hated Sujoy. He had made her work like a slave. At one point in the first three months, their relationship had reached a flashpoint. There was some research required and Sujoy had assigned her the task at 8.00 pm in the night and wanted the report on his desk at 9.00 am the next morning. She had objected and said that it was not possible. That was when Sujoy had played on her ego. He told her, "Nowadays young people don't have the appetite for hard work. I will do it myself." That is when guilt struck her. She picked up the file and said "You will have the report on your desk by 9." She worked through the night and delivered it by 11.00 am. She was rewarded with an out of turn promotion.

Such instances were very frequent over the next few years. It was a combination of hard work, talent and great mentorship that had led to Twisha's meteoric rise. Looking back, Twisha was completely convinced that she deserved every promotion she got.

She would get all the high profile projects. She would be in meetings with people who were two levels her senior. The brashness of youth knows no fear. She was fiery, not afraid to speak the truth and held her own in these meetings, in the presence of some very senior people. All of this created a very favourable impression and led to her climbing the corporate ladder very fast.

However, she had heard murmurs of resentment from her peers. Some of them attributed her meteoric rise to her closeness to Sujoy. She however, ignored all these barbs and comments and focussed on what she could do best.

"Now that you are saying it, maybe yes... some of them." Twisha blurted out.

"That you will move with Sujoy is a foregone conclusion. It is not a matter of whether, but when. These same people who attribute your growth to Sujoy, are expecting you to move with him. And they are also waiting for you to fail, now that Sujoy is out."

"What are you saying?"

"Ok let me ask you something. Who is taking up Sujoy's position?"

"Nobody. The management wants me to do his role."

"Are you sure?"

"Absolutely Karan."

"Good. This means the management has faith in you. While you have people who are expecting you to fail, the management believes in you. Sujoy is not in love with you romantically. He respects you for your talent. And this move by the management, reinforces that. Even they believe in you and your potential. This is actually a great opportunity for you. You can convince the non-believers that you deserve to be here on your own merit. Your performance has to speak for yourself. You have to deliver without Sujoy's protective cover. It doesn't matter whether you succeed or fail, but I am sure that you will succeed. It is only then that people will respect you."

"If you follow Sujoy to the new organisation, there will be murmurs, both here and in the new organisation. A lot of people will say that you have got your Vice President designation only because of Sujoy. Your talent and hard work will be undermined. You will be the package deal that comes with Sujoy. Here the designation might come maybe a year later. But once you get the same, it will be purely on your merit. Then nobody will be able to attribute your growth to your Dronacharya. You will be recognised as a competent archer and warrior. Who knows, tomorrow you may even reach greater heights than Sujoy."

Twisha was silent and did not answer. She just sipped her *chaas* (buttermilk) and became pensive. She cleared the dishes, gave Karan a big hug and went back to her room. She had just found a new respect for Karan.

She knew what to do. She had to find her own path on her own terms. She had a point to prove... to the world.... no.... to herself. Can she step out of her Dronacharya's shadow and succeed? Only time will tell!

But, one thing was for sure, she had outgrown her Dronacharya.

———————∽———————

RECRUITING KARNA

"After the written test, you have a two hour break. In those two hours, I want you to go and change your clothes. I want you to wear those clothes that you are comfortable wearing. Ladies and Gentlemen, we are here to recruit the best minds."

With this Aditi and Priya, left the room.

Aditi and Priya were part of Protective Web Networks (PROWEN), an IT security company. They were visiting an engineering college to recruit for Aditi's department.

PROWEN was highly respected on campus and eagerly awaited. They were not high paying, but the projects that they had were of a high quality. Spending the first five years with PROWEN would catapult people's career into a different orbit.

Aditi was a Vice President in charge of an innovation department called 'Disruptive Technologies.' The best minds worked here and were responsible for the next generation of ideas and technologies. Getting into this department was extremely difficult. Aditi had personally recruited everybody. They would either be handpicked or would go through an interview with Aditi.

A couple of months ago, Aditi decided that she needed fresh brains, and even stated that she would accompany HR to the campus in Rohtak. On hearing this, HR flipped. They knew Aditi's maverick ways, and were unhappy about taking her along. Aditi wanted the best talent, and this was actually a Tier 3 college. They wondered how Aditi would find top talent in a small place. They were also worried about how Aditi would behave on campus. Not that she would run around naked or something of that sort, but they were sure she would do something very unconventional. The other problem was that given Aditi's maverick reputation, they wondered who in HR would be able to manage her.

Priya had recently graduated from Symbiosis, Pune and joined the recruitment team in PROWEN. She was fresh out of B-School and was just finding her roots in recruitment. She was 'volunteered' to join Aditi in the recruitment team. The moment Priya got the news that she had to visit Rohtak with Aditi, she was overjoyed. This was her first 'official tour', and like most newcomers, she was excited. She was also tense as Aditi was a stickler for perfection and everybody was scared of her. She was honoured that a junior analyst like her would be spending a couple of days with Aditi. What she did not know was that she was being sent simply because no one else wanted to go.

Sure enough, Aditi started displaying her temperament right from the moment they landed at the Railway station. Even though there was a car to pick them up, she asked Priya to go ahead and said that she would come in an auto. Priya had no clue how to deal with the situation. The Vice President would catch an auto while a junior analyst would travel by car?! She wondered whether she should accompany Aditi in the auto, but before she could say anything, Aditi had disappeared. Priya was greeted by Rahul, a final year student and the college placement cell representative, who would accompany her in the car during the journey to campus.

Six months ago, she had been on the other side, in Symbiosis, escorting corporate executives to campus, accompanying them to dinner etc. and here she was today, as a recruiter. She was excited, but a part of her brain was thinking of Aditi. What kind of lady disappears in an auto in a strange place where there's a pick up facility? What would Priya do if something happened to Aditi? Even though Aditi was much elder to her, she was attractive and thirty five years young. Rahul indulged in small talk about the journey etc. but Priya could not concentrate on the same. She decided to call Aditi.

"Aditi madam, where are you? Are you fine?"

"Chill sweetheart, everything is fine, I am enjoying Rohtak. And you don't call me madam."

"Yes madam."

Aditi laughed and hung up the phone.

Priya did not know what to do. She then decided to take the matter into her own hands. She would deal with the consequences later. She called Aditi once again.

"Now what's the matter dear?"

"Listen Aditi, we are in a different town and both of us need to take responsibility for each other. You can go in your auto rickshaw anywhere, but this is what I want you to do. You will tell me your co-ordinates right now and stop. My car will reach that place, and follow you. You can do whatever you want but under surveillance." Priya was polite but extremely stern while saying this.

"Aha, so we have a tigress in HR. Are you requesting me dear or instructing me? I am five levels your senior, do you know the repercussions if I complain against you?"

"Aditi, this is an order not a request. And if you are going to complain, it's completely your prerogative, I don't care." Priya's parents were in the armed forces, she knew the importance of authority and listening to seniors. But she was extremely clear that when situation warranted, even seniors had to be ordered. Children from a defence background clearly know when to be firm; it is part of their DNA. She was actually angry at the way Aditi spoke to her on the phone and hence had used the word 'order' instead of 'instruction.' Now she knew why everybody was scared of Aditi. She thought Aditi was extremely haughty and snobbish.

"Well, if HR orders one has to obey. Listen, meet me at Bara Bazaar in 10 minutes."

Priya reached Bara Bazaar only to see Aditi, eating Gajar ka Halwa with the auto driver.

"*Arey teen aur plate dena.* Priya, Gajar ka Halwa is famous here. Call the driver too." Priya could not believe what she was seeing. Ten minutes ago, Aditi had played the 'power of position' card with her, and now she was eating with the auto driver. In fact, she was busy talking to the driver, some other locals, and completely ignored Priya. After a few minutes, Aditi paid the auto driver and joined them in the car and started chatting with Rahul, the placement co-ordinator. It was as if Priya was non-existent. Well, if she wanted to act snobbish, so be it.

On reaching campus, Aditi's behaviour changed. She was like a general barking out orders. Priya was ready and well prepared with the material. That is when Aditi took out another envelope from her bag.

"Priya, please keep your question papers in the bag, I don't need them. Hand these out." Priya was stumped, however she was half expecting something like this. She did as she was told, and while handing the papers out, took a glance at them. There was just one question on each page.

'*Q1. Name three current products which will not exist five years from now*

'*Q2. Please narrate an experience where you have experienced failure*'

Priya was gaping at the questions. Was this a joke or was Aditi looking for bright minds? Suddenly Rahul approached Aditi, "Madam these are the Resumes of the candidates."

Shit. Disaster! Priya had heard that Aditi was famous for tearing up resumes. During interviews, people would give her their resume, and she would tear it up in front of them. By the time they came out of the shock of their resume being torn up, the interview was over. Priya was specifically warned of this and aware of the scene Aditi could create.

"Here Rahul, please give them to me. And can you help me to the washroom please?"

Aditi looked at both of them and smiled. Smart kid, she thought.

"Rahul, listen to this very carefully. Please take back all the resumes. Remember, if any student wants to be recruited, they are not to, repeat, not to get into the interview room with their resumes. Is that crystal clear?"

"Yes ma'am." Rahul was already in awe of Priya, as he had heard her order Aditi around in the car. He quickly realised that this was a different recruitment process.

Aditi finished giving instructions and both of them got into a room. Priya was angry with Aditi; she did not understand what this lady was up to. She had been part of the campus placement team in her college for the final two years before graduation and had seen multiple companies in action, but hadn't seen any process like this. She had heard that nobody wanted to accompany Aditi, and now she knew why. Aditi's methods were too unconventional for others to understand. She was too whimsical for other people to tolerate her. Was that the case, or was there a method to the madness? After all one doesn't become a Vice President at 32 working on whims and fancies. Priya was sure this trip would be among the biggest learning experiences of her career.

"I am sorry Priya, I talked arrogantly to you on the phone."

Priya could not believe her ears. Thirty minutes ago, this lady was threatening her with dire consequences, and now the same lady was apologising to her? Gajar ka Halwa actually produced heat in the body, but it had cooled down Aditi. Maybe it was the winter of North India!

"It's okay madam." Priya was still unsure what to make of the apology.

From Priya's body language, Aditi understood that she was not happy with the conversation that took place during the auto ride. She got up, hugged Priya and smiled.

"You know I have been unfair to you. I gave you grief on the phone but I didn't intend to, I was testing you. Firstly we are not used to taking orders from HR, not because we have a superiority complex, but we have observed that HR has no spine. And here, we have a tigress having the courage to speak sternly to a colleague who is five levels her senior, within the first three months of her corporate career. I was actually happy, but wanted to test you a bit more before forming an opinion. And you have passed the test with flying colours."

"Thanks Aditi, I am sorry I misunderstood you and already formed a judgement about you."

"Never ever pass any value judgements about people. Have you read the Mahabharata?"

"Parts of it."

"Do you know that Duryodhana was a righteous king?"

"You are kidding, Duryodhana?"

"The Mahabharata war happened very close to where we are. However, do you know that there is a Duryodhana temple in Kollam in Kerala?"

"I don't believe this. I always thought he was the villain. How come I don't know about it even though I am from Kerala?" Priya was a Palghat Iyer, a Tamilian, from Kerala.

"Perspectives dear, perspectives. Both of us had two different perspectives of the same conversation which happened half an hour ago. I could understand your perspective and how you thought, simply because of my experience. However as you did not have my perspective, you painted me a villain and thought that I am snobbish."

"You are amazing Aditi, but not a difficult person to work with. Why is everybody in HR afraid of you?"

"Simple Priya, I wear my heart on my sleeve and I don't suffer fools. Hence people think I am not empathetic and don't want to work with me. However if you speak to the people in my team, you will realise that we are a family. We fight like dogs, but each fight is just professional. Personally we just love each other and respect each other."

"When you ordered me, you did the right thing. I was foolish to run away in an unknown city, but realised my mistake when you called. I actually liked the way you ordered me and your choice of words reminded me of myself ten years ago."

Aditi had just paid Priya a huge compliment. Priya realised that, what people thought was a 'difficult assignment', was in fact a golden opportunity. She just had to pick Aditi's brains and understand her thought process.

"What is the rationale behind the two questions?"

"I was waiting for you to ask this. You know I am recruiting for my team which is called 'Disruptive Technologies.' I need brains which think and not which code. My question is going to make them think. No book or preparation is going to help them answer this."

"And failure?"

"This is actually the most important question. In resumes people highlight their achievements. I want to know, how many people have gone through failure and then have the guts to stand up and admit the same."

"But why? Is it that people who can stand up after failing have a good temperament?"

"You seem to be watching too many Harsha Bhogle videos on YouTube. My reason is different. Innovation is not about success, but about failure. When you innovate, you start with complete belief and passion towards your product. Rarely does one get a great new product on the first try. Somewhere in between, you realise how stupid your work has been. That is what I call a light-bulb moment. Once you realise that, you have to quickly put your hand up and accept failure, so your next attempt is better. I need people who are not bogged down by failure."

"Interesting!"

"Our educational system inculcates the spirit of success. Nothing wrong with that, but they don't teach you how to handle failure. We are a risk management company. Why do risks arise? It is because people are not encouraged to highlight failures. Remember, to err is human. If so, then why do corporates penalise people for mistakes which are human? Even Performance Management Systems penalise people every time they fail, hence it is not in their best interests to highlight their failure which is shoved under the carpet, leading to risks. There needs to be a culture of honesty without fear of reprimand in any organisation. One is right or wrong only in hindsight. But the importance of recognising the same before the damage is done is important. Do you know Priya that every time there is an acknowledged failure, we celebrate it with a party?"

"What?! No wonder they call you maverick."

"There is a reason Priya. I am suspicious of success, especially if it comes very early. It means that some simple fatal flaw has been overlooked. I love failure, because once the reasons are documented, everybody in the team learns from the same. Success is just a logical outcome of failure. So when I look at the answer sheets today, I check it from failures first."

"Now I know why you tear resumes!"

Aditi smiled. This kid was good and learning fast.

Rahul came in with the answer sheets.

"Now that you know what I am looking for, you can start checking. Look at the answer to the failure question, if it is blank, throw away the candidature." Aditi minced no words.

Out of seventy five, they could shortlist only eight candidates. Aditi gave the list to Rahul and asked him for directions to the college canteen.

"Please let us know, what you want, we will get it for you here." Rahul said.

By now Aditi's actions had ceased to shock Priya. She laughed and chided herself at not having predicted this move by Aditi.

"No Rahul, we insist on going to the canteen alone. We will commence interviews at 2.00 pm in this room."

They had lunch in the canteen and chatted with the students. All along, Priya observed how Aditi had made all the youngsters comfortable and engaged in a free flowing conversation with them.

At the scheduled hour of 2.00 p.m., they commenced interviews. By the time they had interviewed five candidates, Aditi was wondering whether it had been a mistake to come to Rohtak.

The next student was Yogesh.

Yogesh entered the room in a swagger, dressed in Khaki trousers and a blue shirt. The shirt was crumpled and sweaty and the pocket had an ink stain. His shoes were unpolished, as a matter of fact, there were stitches on the outer half of the left shoe, where it had been patched up and it was plainly visible.

"You begin." Aditi nudged Priya.

Priya was actually shocked at Yogesh's appearance. Coming from a defence background, proper appearance was mandatory. While it would not be anything flashy, shoes would always be polished, clothes would always be ironed, and she would always turn out very smart. Here was a guy appearing for a job interview, and he come in crumpled clothes. She had noticed the sewn shoes before, and realised that while writing the test he had worn a coat.

While other candidates had turned out in jeans, he had come in the same formals.

"Are you comfortable in these clothes?" Priya asked.

"No."

"We asked you to go and change, why did you not do so?"

"Stay far."

Priya was wondering why this guy was giving very short answers.

"Why does your shirt have a blue stain?"

"*Kya farak padta hain? Interview mera le rahe ho ya shirt ka*" Yogesh barked. (What difference does it make, are you interviewing me or the shirt?)

Aditi realised that Priya had touched some raw nerve. She placed her hand on Priya's lap and signalled that she would take over.

"Your failure is that you lost in the first round in the inter-collegiate badminton championship. Why did you lose that match?"

"Play ... better." Yogesh mentioned in broken English.

"I don't see any other badminton related failures after that. Did you give up badminton?"

"I win Inter Collegiate Championship three years."

By now it was apparent that Yogesh was struggling with English. Aditi noticed this quickly and conducted the rest of the interview in Hindi. That is when Yogesh came into his element.

He had a free flowing conversation with Aditi in Hindi.

"So Yogesh, you have written that news will disappear in the next 5 years, but newspapers will stay, can you explain?"

"Madam what we get today are not newspapers, but advertorials, with news thrown in for you to feel that it is a newspaper. In five years, newspapers will have more advertisements than news. This is due to the internet."

"Aren't you contradicting yourself Yogesh?"

"No I am not. It is very funny, news has shifted to the internet, while advertisements are gaining ground in the print media. If you realise, magazines, which have a strong detailed content, have moved online."

"But the online space is littered with advertisements."

"I am sorry madam, it is the other way around. Flipkart launches their big sale, and does a two page advertisement in the newspaper. Myntra goes off the computer to the tablet, and you have a two page ad on that. Every product launch is jointly present both in the online as well as print market. Also online ads can be skipped, print ads can't be. They are just visible and in your face. Online ads are visible to only one set of eyeballs, which visits the website, but print ads are visible to everybody including the kid in the house. Print ads help in considerable brand building."

Aditi fell in love with Yogesh. She immediately knew that she wanted him for the team. Priya did not like the selection, but she knew enough about Aditi to not object then and there. She would take up the matter over dinner.

After the interviews, Priya and Aditi went out for dinner to a nearby restaurant. Priya was a vegetarian, and Aditi also decided to order vegetarian food.

"So Priya what do you think of Yogesh?"

"He is good."

"No Priya, he is not good, he is very good."

"But Aditi, he can't speak English to save his life."

"Why am I not surprised by this question Priya? I thought you were different and started liking you. But HR will be HR."

"Now who is passing a value judgement?"

Aditi had raised the glass to drink water and she spluttered. "What did you just say?"

"I said, 'who is passing a value judgement?'."

"Priya, you are better than I imagined." Aditi bowed down in front of her and said "Respect". Priya was thoroughly embarrassed.

"Since you talk about value judgements, let's go back to Duryodhana's story. Does caste system still exist in India today?"

"I would want to believe it does not, but it does. They say that in some states of India, people don't cast their vote, but vote their caste. How is this connected to Duryodhana's story?"

"Do you know Duryodhana did not believe in the caste system even then?"

"Wow, amazing! Nobody knows this about Duryodhana."

"It was the graduation ceremony of the princes of the Kuru clan. The princes who had learnt with Dronacharya would display their skills, in the presence of the elders of the Kuru dynasty and the commoners. It was in a stadium. Duryodhana who was an expert in the maze displayed his skill. However the scene stealer was Arjuna. He displayed his amazing archery skills. He would shoot blindfolded at the source of sound. It was a foregone conclusion that Arjuna would get the best performer's prize. Suddenly a masked youth entered the stadium and proceeded to display all the tricks that Arjuna had done, only he did them better. No one knew the identity of the youth. However, he had managed to impress one and all. The popular vote about the best performer was with him. Suddenly a gust of wind blew away his mask. He was Karna the charioteer's son."

"What a story!!"

"This is the interesting part. He had gate-crashed the competition, he did not have an invitation to the party. Should he have been disqualified?"

"Good question, very difficult to answer."

"Priya, the competition was for the Kuru princes, he was a charioteer's son, and he had no business entering the competition."

"That's discrimination Aditi. The art of war is not a prerogative of kings and princes. So did he get the prize for the best performer?"

"So you agree, that discrimination against somebody based on his background, is not right?"

"Of course it isn't."

"So should we give Yogesh a chance to enter the competition?"

Suddenly the meaning of the entire story hit Priya. Yogesh did not come from a fancy background. He was from a small city. Should he not be given a chance to compete with the big boys? Aditi had a point. And it was an interesting way in which she made it.

"Aditi, I have no issues about Yogesh's skills. He is a bright chap. But let us accept the fact that the entire office speaks in English. Yogesh should be recruited and set up for success, but my question is are we setting him up for failure?"

"Fair point. Let me tell you what happened in the competition. Dronacharya who was one of the judges said that competition happens only among equals. As Karna was not from a princely family, there was no way he could be awarded the prize."

"How ridiculous."

"This is where Duryodhana stepped up. He was the crown prince. Then and there, on the spot, he crowned Karna prince of Anga, thereby making him an equal."

"Amazing... and they say Duryodhana was a villain. What a great act by him."

"Can you think Priya, why did Duryodhana crown Karna as prince of Anga?"

"He thought Karna was the fair winner, and hence he was on the side of what was right."

"You are correct Priya, but there are other elements which are extremely important. Firstly, there was a massive rivalry between the Kauravas and the Pandavas. Duryodhana had foresight that at some point there would be a war between them. Arjuna was a great archer, but there wasn't anybody who was a counter to him. When Karna bettered Arjuna, Duryodhana was quick to spot his talent. He realised that Karna was a great archer, and importantly, here was someone who could be a valid counter to Arjuna."

"Aditi, I will never forget this trip to Rohtak. I am learning from you every minute."

"So what did Duryodhana do when he crowned Karna prince of Anga?"

"He made him the prince, what else?"

"Think Priya think...."

Priya now contemplated and went over the entire story once again. "Duryodhana made Karna an equal."

"What was missing from Karna's qualifications? That did not allow him to win the competition?"

"He was not a Royal...."

"Priya, by gifting him the kingdom of Anga, Duryodhana made him a Royal."

Elementary, Priya thought. She was still thinking at a higher level and here was Aditi, breaking the episode into fragments and analysing them. But... hang on, was Aditi just telling a fancy story? If so, why this detailed analysis... suddenly the meaning of the entire story struck her. The roti fell from her hands as she realised what Aditi meant.

Aditi smiled. She knew that Priya had understood the meaning.

"So Aditi, did they give the award to Karna?"

"Unfortunately no. Kunti, Pandavas' mother, suddenly fainted in the VIP enclosure. In the commotion that ensued, Dronacharya announced the award for Arjuna, and the story ended there."

"How cunning of Dronacharya. But why did Kunti faint, was it because of the heat?"

"No sweetheart, Kunti recognised Karna as her son, whom she had abandoned at birth, as she was an unwed mother at that time."

"What, Karna was Kunti's son?"

"Yes and the eldest among both the Kauravas and Pandavas," replied Aditi and then asked Priya, "So, are we going to recruit our Karna?"

———～———

ARJUNA'S MISTAKE

"Friends, New York has ordered us to cut costs. I have promised a twenty percent reduction in our budgets for the rest of the year. I want you all to go back to your respective departments and look at what can be reduced. Shraddha, the finance head, and I will review the budgets with you next week. I look forward to concrete proposals from you." With this Mahesh adjourned the meeting. He knew it was a tough task, like squeezing blood from stone but still they had to do it. After all New York was the boss.

Mahesh was the head of India operations, of the back office of an international bank headquartered in New York. He had just moved from London to Mumbai three months ago and cost cutting was one of the first items on his agenda. It was a tough year for banking across the globe. Banks were just coming out of the 2008 financial crisis, however events across the world weren't helping. Growth across the globe was slow to non-existent. China's growth was slowing down and commodity prices across the globe had collapsed. In an election year, Wall Street definitely wasn't part of the politicians' guest list. People in the US were already angry about the 2008 bailout of Wall Street, especially when the average person on the street was unemployed and fancy bonuses were being paid to top executives of banks. Scandals and huge losses from Wall Street showed no signs of abating.

On top of that, regulators were breathing down their neck. There was the controversial Volcker rule, which had the potential of eating away twenty five percent of the banks' revenues. Basel rules were getting stringent by the day and there was huge pressure on both capital and revenues[1]. If the firm had to retain its profitability, costs had to be controlled, there was no choice.

Mandar, who was head of the transport department, was very worried. He knew that costs were already cut to the bone. He was very well known across the organisation and had a personal equation with a lot of people. He decided to speak to Vinita from finance and see if she could help. He called her for a cup of coffee.

"Vinita, as you are aware there is a massive cost cutting initiative across the organisation. As part of that our budgets are going to be cut by twenty percent. They are already cut to the bone. Can you help me analyse the numbers and see what kind of proposal I can go to Mahesh with?"

Vinita looked at the numbers and called back.

---

[1] Basel is a city in Switzerland, where Central Bankers from the world met in 1998 and published a set of minimum capital requirements for banks. These have been colloquially called as Basel rules. Since the financial crisis in 2008, the regulators have been turning screws on banks and the latest set of rules, called Basel III are extremely stringent

"Mandar I have gone through your numbers. There is a very interesting trend. Your ad hoc transport costs are nearly thirty percent of total costs. See if you can reduce that."

Mandar knew what Vinita was talking about. If she had pointed this out after just a cursory glance, it would definitely not escape Mahesh and Shraddha's attention. He was dreading the conversation with Mahesh and Shraddha next week.

*****

The India back office team worked 24 X 7. People worked in different shifts and the organisation functioned throughout the day and night. The current Back Offices, Call centres, where people work in different shifts are no different from factories of 30 years ago, where production ran in three shifts. There was just one difference – in factories, there were very few women working in night shifts. The impact of globalisation and modernity was that in these call centres and back offices, everybody worked every shift irrespective of gender. People would leave the office after their work was over, which could mean 1.00 am or 2.30 am or even 4.00 am. In order to ensure that people felt comfortable and safe, there was a drop system in place. Every employee leaving office after a certain hour would be dropped home in a cab. People staying in the same locality would be clubbed together. No woman who would be dropped last would travel alone with the driver.

There would be a security guard who would be her escort. Everybody would have to be dropped at their doorstep.

The transport department was in charge of arranging cabs for these drops. It was a massive exercise in logistics. Just because the organisation arranged cabs for people to go home, it wasn't at people's will. There were specified drop times for which people had to enrol at least one hour prior to the drop. Based on the number of people who enrolled, and as per their residential addresses, the transport department would plan out the routes and arrange for the required number of cabs. The challenge just began there. Even if 40 people would have registered for drops, there would be five who would drop out and another seven who would turn up un-registered.

It was not that people abused the system. The registration would close one hour before. People in the middle of their work would forget registering, or miss the deadline to register by a few minutes. In some cases, even if they had registered for a drop, their estimate of when their work will end would be wrong, thus they would over shoot their departure time and miss the drop. In other situations, there would be a last minute request from New York, which would force them to miss the drop they had enrolled for and for the next drop, they would be un-registered.

The transport department was at its wits' end as to how to manage this. It was a logistics nightmare. Based on the registrations, they would arrange for a certain number of cabs. Some cabs would go unutilised, at other times they would have to order a few cabs at the last minute. In case cabs were ordered at the last minute, the vendor would charge them a twenty five percent premium. This premium was billed separately and would show up as ad-hoc charges.

In order to curb this, the transport department had framed a policy to charge the actual cost of transport to the departments. Dropouts would be billed at double the standard rate. Last minute unregistered drops would be accommodated to the extent possible. They would also be billed at double the standard rate.

This billing system generated huge controversy. Departments faced with cost pressures would engage in constant battles with the transport department, and even pressurise them to reduce the charges for dropouts and unregistered drops. As head of the transport department, Mandar stood his ground. He said, if you want to reduce costs, reduce dropouts and unregistered drops.

*****

It was 2.30 am and Neelam Mehra had just rushed to the basement to get into the cab. She had worked non-stop for nearly 13 hours. She was tired and looking forward to going home. Unfortunately she had not registered for the drop and was wondering whether she would get one. If she did not get the drop, she would have to wait for one more hour as the next drop was only at 3.30. At the same time, Kritika a Vice President was also waiting for the drop. Neelam went across to Kritika and explained her situation. Kritika assured her that she would ensure that Neelam would get the drop. As Neelam had feared, there was no place for her in the cab. The transport representative requested her to take the next drop.

What followed was a massive war of words. Kritika ensured that Neelam got the drop in her place. She called her husband in the middle of the night to come over and pick her up. Kritika was angry and mad. This episode was escalated the next day and Mandar was summoned and given a dressing down.

Mandar immediately called up his team and issued verbal instructions that nobody was to be refused a drop at night, even if they were not registered. If additional cabs had to be called so be it.

*****

Mandar's meeting with Mahesh and Shraddha was on Monday. Unfortunately Mahesh could not make it so Shraddha chaired the meeting. The outcome was as expected. He was instructed to cut down on the ad hoc costs, as they were not part of the policy. Mandar protested that it was difficult to avoid ad hoc costs. Shraddha documented the minutes of the meeting by sending the following email to Mahesh and Mandar.

"It is observed that the ad hoc costs of the transport department are nearly thirty percent of total costs. As these costs are due to employees violating the transport policy, you are instructed to reduce this cost and ensure there are no policy violations."

Mandar read the email and filed it away.

*****

Four weeks later Mahesh received the cost report. What he saw alarmed him. The transport department's costs did not seem to be going down. Shraddha's email was self-explanatory.

"The ad hoc costs of the transport department which are against policy are actually up by another twenty percent. Please ensure that they come down."

It was time for a showdown with Mandar. Mahesh forwarded Shraddha's mail to Mandar.

"Mandar – Please refer to Shraddha's mail. You need to understand that the cost needs to go down. If your costs are up due to policy violations, you need to seek prior approval before that cost is approved. Given the environment, it is just not possible that we can approve any exceptions."

Mandar replied back,

"Mahesh – Thanks for your email. I understand the situation on costs. However the circumstances are such that we cannot avoid them. It is also not possible to seek prior approval for these policy violations. I would like to meet up with you in person and explain the situation."

Mahesh was irritated at this reply. This was a clear case of insubordination. This guy had the cheek to refuse orders and even refused to seek prior approval. He seemed to be stubborn. Maybe it was time for Mandar to go. If somebody does not understand the organisation's compulsions and still violates policy, they deserve a punishment. While he was thinking along these lines, his phone rang.

"Are you coming to the movie? If so, then you need to leave right now." Mahesh had promised to take his wife to the new Khan movie followed by dinner. This was one of their monthly rituals. One Friday (or more if possible) every month, he would leave early, watch the latest Bollywood release followed by dinner with his wife. Their children were grown up and at a stage where they rarely went out with their parents.

Post the movie, Mahesh and his wife Deepa were having a quiet dinner at Palladium. Suddenly there was a noise and a group of youngsters entered. Everybody started looking at the source of the noise.

"Stop ogling at girls half your age," Deepa teased Mahesh.

"That's all I can do... ogle at them."

"I am sure you want to do more than ogle at them." Deepa was in the mood for some banter.

"Yes, but I can't do anything else."

"Hmm. Somebody's growing old."

"It's not that I am growing old. It is not worth sacrificing a lifetime of happiness for a few minutes of pleasure. The payoff is just not worth it."

"Oh really? So you mean to say, you still are young and have the energy?"

"Do you know Deepa… that human beings are not meant to be monogamous?"

"Now don't give me a philosophical explanation for your fantasies."

"Seriously Deepa, we are mammals and part of the animal chain. Are animals monogamous?"

"So you want to be in a polygamous society? And what are your views on polyandry?"

"Well, Draupadi practised polyandry."

"She was forced to… Mahesh. Arjuna won her hand in marriage, and when he brought her home, he said, like a child 'Look ma, what I have got'. And Kunti without looking back, said, 'Whatever you have got, share it with your brothers.'"

"Wonder how the arrangement worked."

"Surprising you don't know Mahesh. Draupadi had a separate chamber, and would live with one of the brothers one year at a time. None of the other brothers was supposed to enter her chamber if Draupadi was present with one of her husbands."

"Interesting. Were there any penalties for violations?"

"If the privacy was violated, the offending party would live in exile in the forest for twelve years. Each of the brothers had taken an oath specifying this in front of sage Narada"

"And was there a violation?"

"There was one violation. One day a Brahmin came to Arjuna and said that somebody was running away with his cattle and asked Arjuna's help. Arjuna wanted to help him, but his bow and arrow were in Draupadi's chamber. At that time, Yudhisthir was in Draupadi's chamber. Arjuna entered the chamber, picked up his bow and arrow and went away. He did his duty."

"So, was he punished for this offence?"

"Mr. Managing Director, why don't you answer this question, whether he should have been punished?"

"This is a very tricky one Deepa."

"Ok so you are head of your organisation and are asked to sit on judgement on this one, what would you do?"

Deepa's statement hit Mahesh strongly. Just before leaving his office that day, he was to sit on judgement on somebody who had violated policy. The similarity of the situations suddenly dawned on Mahesh.

"Ok, so here is my argument. If there is a violation of policy, there has to be a punishment." Mahesh answered casually.

Mahesh's statement infuriated Deepa. She had begun her career as an analyst in an IT company, and grown up the ranks. She had moved from Programming, to Project Management, to Sales and even had a stint in HR. She had done 15 years in her career, before giving it up in order to accompany Mahesh to London. Now she dabbled in philanthropy and worked closely with an NGO involved in the education sector. She had seen various policies implemented and fought against some of them which were prehistoric and just did not make sense. She had won some battles in her careers, lost quite a few. In the process she created some enemies and lots of admirers. She was not going to let this statement pass unchallenged

"Good Mahesh, who makes the policies?"

"Obviously the organisation does. Each policy is made with a bigger purpose in mind."

"Exactly, the 'one brother – one year policy' was made to ensure that after Draupadi's marriage to five brothers they respected her and her privacy. Firstly, the brothers had put her in an awkward position by getting her married to five people instead of one. Would you tolerate it if our daughter ran away with her boyfriend and reached their home, only to be told by their mother, to share her with his brothers? How much more ridiculous can it get?!" Deepa was animated and speaking from her heart. Whenever Deepa was in this mood, her tone and pitch would go up.

"Chill Deepa. Don't talk too loudly about the wrongs in the Mahabharata, especially by the Pandavas. Religious fundamentalism is alive in this country."

Deepa quietened down and laughed.

"You know Deepa, there is another reason why this policy was created. When two or more men are in love with one woman, they are bound to destroy each other. Here we have a case where five men are getting married to one lady, in case a fair arrangement had not been worked out, it would be but natural that they would end up destroying each other."

"Good! So now that the bigger purpose has been established, Mahesh, should Arjuna be punished?"

"In this case, Arjuna entered the chamber not with the intention of invading Draupadi and Yudhishthir's privacy, but for the purpose of picking his bow, which was needed immediately at that time. It could not wait. Hence he should not be punished."

"Good point Mahesh. But do organisations follow this policy? There are layers in every organisation. Sometimes, a decision is taken at the senior most level, but is not understood at junior levels. Actually if you talk to people with a few years' experience at junior levels, they will tell you how ridiculous some policies are. And then these people bear the brunt for the policy violation, not because it is their fault, but the policy doesn't make sense."

"Your anger towards the Pandavas seems to have been channelled towards the Corporates!!"

"It is not anger... it is just a matter of fact... we got into this conversation that triggered something that I feel strongly about. Tell me Mahesh, how many times have you understood the circumstances that led to a policy violation and subsequent disciplinary action?"

"Deepa, if I have to sit in for every disciplinary hearing, what are processes for?"

"Processes are inhuman Mahesh. If you think people are your biggest asset, should they be disciplined by processes or people?" Deepa thundered.

"Deepa, I, as a Managing Director cannot be expected to attend every disciplinary hearing. I have my stakeholders." Mahesh knew what Deepa was saying made sense and he was fighting a losing battle. However the solution wasn't easy.

"Aren't your employees your stakeholders Mahesh? Or is it only your bosses, who pay your salary?"

"Extremely sorry dear! As usual you win. For the last twenty five years I haven't been able to win any logical debate with you."

Twenty five years ago, was the first time when Mahesh and Deepa faced off in a debate in the run up to the Student

Council elections. Deepa had won the debate then and continued to win these debates. Mahesh actually enjoyed these debates, as Deepa always talked sense. Throughout the last twenty years, Mahesh actually took something from these debates and implemented it at the workplace. He was appreciated for his innovative ideas and people friendly approach, but he attributed more than half of his success to Deepa. During these debates, Deepa would come up with some kind of innovation or people practice, which Mahesh would be quick to pick and relate to the corporate environment and apply it.

"So Mahesh, should employees be disciplined for policy violations?"

"Deepa, I will be candid. If I were asked this question without context, I would have said yes. However after listening to Arjuna's story, I believe that if there is a greater good that is to be achieved from the violation, the violation does not need to be punished. As a matter of fact, exceptions to the rules need to be created."

"That's the smart chap I fell in love with twenty five years ago," said Deepa with a beaming smile.

"And that's the intelligent woman, I fell in love with twenty five years ago." Mahesh smiled back.

"Thanks for the compliment, Mahesh, but if I remember right, you fell in love with the beautiful girl and not the intelligence."

"Beautiful and fiery, after all you were the one who ended my unbeaten run."

Deepa had defeated Mahesh in a closely fought Students Council election by three votes.

"So did you lose to my beauty or brains?"

"I lost the election, but won the battle of life."

"Cheers to that." Both of them lifted their glasses of Malbec and clinked them in a toast to each other.

"By the way, did Arjuna get punished?"

"Yes, he had to spend twelve years in the forest for his violation."

*****

Mahesh reached office on Monday morning, and asked for background information on Mandar. He was impressed with what he saw. Mandar had good ratings, everybody had good things to say about him and he was well respected. Mahesh realised that his refusal to reduce the ad-hoc transport costs, must have a reason.

He also called for the transport policy which was being violated. He decided to talk to Mandar and understand his perspective. After all rarely does one refuse the big boss' order and that too by email. The normal behaviour that he had seen was that people would agree to his orders and if targets were not achieved, apologise and make excuses. Mandar seemed to come from a different breed.

"So Mandar, I see that the transport policy has been drafted by you."

"Yes sir."

"And you are violating the same. Isn't that a paradox? You are violating your own rules?"

"Let me explain sir." Mandar then went on to narrate the Neelam Mehra episode.

"Mahesh, if I turn you away at 2:30 am in the night, only because you haven't registered for the drop, what will your reaction be?"

"I will be extremely angry."

"Will you wait for the 3:30 am drop? Remember you have put in nearly 14 hours of work"

"Not a chance in hell. I will curse you and go home by auto."

"What if you are a lady sir, will you stay till 3:30 am or go home by auto?"

"Difficult question to answer Mandar."

"Let me tell you what happens sir. Even ladies travel alone at night. Mumbai has the reputation of being a safe city. These people have put in 14 hours of work. Some of them are young mothers. Their child is waiting for them at home. In some cases, they have to wake up early, do the housework for family members who work normal India timings and then leave for work. The least they would like is to go home promptly at the end of day's work."

"Good point Mandar."

"Firstly, sir, if our people are working twelve to fourteen hours every day, and we have promised them a drop, we need to give them a drop, irrespective of the cost. Sir, when Kritika escalated the Neelam Mehra incident, I came to my senses. We have been extremely lucky that there has been no untoward incident so far. I have given verbal instructions to my staff to ensure that nobody is turned back for a cab, if they have not registered, irrespective of the cost. We should accommodate everybody at that hour, irrespective of gender. And if you want prior approval, I will ask my staff to call you directly at 2:30 am. If you don't pick up the call within three rings, it will be considered deemed approval. I cannot hold the cabs back."

All this while, Mahesh had kept his pen on the table and was reclining in his chair with a smile on his face. He had realised that Mandar was acting like Arjuna, for the good of the people and the organisation.

"Mandar, thanks for rejecting my instructions on email. Safety of employees is of paramount importance, irrespective of the cost involved. I like the fire in you, the practice as mentioned by you shall continue. But tell me should we not scrap the policy?"

"Valid point sir, but I will not recommend that. If we scrap the policy entirely, it will send a signal that anything is acceptable. The policy is a deterrent and a reminder to people to register. This will help in the planning exercise. Otherwise scheduling will be a nightmare and the ad hoc costs will go up hugely."

"Point taken Mandar. What you are advocating is a practice which is a deviation from the policy. Both of us are not going to be in the same jobs forever. Tomorrow, if someone comes in your place and decides to follow the policy to the 'T', we could be in for trouble. Or if I move on, and my successor doesn't understand your story, that's another recipe for disaster."

"So what do we do sir?"

"Here's what we will do. I will write you an email, asking you to explain why the transport policy is not being followed, and ad hoc costs not controlled."

"But sir…" Mandar protested.

Mahesh silenced him with a wave of his hand.

"You will write back giving detailed reasons why we need to provide drops to everybody, irrespective of whether they have registered or not. I will then approve the email and give you a blanket permission. You have to take a printout of that email and hand it over to your team. By this we are documenting the reason for the deviation from the policy as well as the right practice. This email will provide a guiding light for both of our successors. In spite of this, if some idiot in your or my place decides to revoke this practice in the future, then I think they will be clearing the decks for their funeral.

Mandar smiled. He now knew why Mahesh had been moved to India and was happy that the centre was in good hands.

BHISHMA'S SILENCE

Vishal parked his car in the parking lot. It was seven in the evening and he was home early. He picked up his laptop, entered the apartment building and climbed up four stories to his residence. His apartment had an elevator, but he walked up the stairs every evening. After all, this was the only exercise he could manage to get in the entire day.

"What a surprise!! Is everything fine?" Ritu was happy that Vishal had come home early.

"I thought I will spend some time with my second wife." This was a common joke between Ritu and Vishal. Due to the amount of time Vishal spent in office, Ritu complained that Vishal was married to his job and she was his second wife.

Ritu and Vishal had met at campus. It was love at first sight, and within two months they were inseparable. At the end of two years, both had obtained an MBA as well as a life partner. Three years after graduating, and working in different cities, they got married. Both came from middle class backgrounds and the fire to succeed was intense. Five years of marriage passed by quickly and before they realised it, they were close to hitting thirty.

In Indian marriages, parents expect "fruits" in the first few years. Ritu's father believed that early marriage followed by early children is good economics. It was not a regressive mind-set, but a more practical one. He believed that you should have children by the age of twenty five. The Indian family ethos believes that if you give good education to your children, they can then fly on their own. These financial responsibilities will peak between the ages of sixteen and twenty two of the children, when parents will be in their mid-forties. Post that, the children can fend for themselves, and the parents have a good 10 years of their career left to save for retirement.

Every time Ritu's parents visited them, Ritu's father would counsel them about this. However Vishal and Ritu were caught in the EMI trap. They had bought a new house, two fancy cars, one for each and had an expensive lifestyle. Vishal argued that when they have children, he would want to spend quality time with them. Currently this was not possible with their hectic work schedules. Given the success they had, and their lifestyles, they also needed the double income.

Five years into the marriage, the "accident" happened. Even though Vishal and Ritu had used protection, the hand of God played its part. The moment Ritu discovered her pregnancy, she decided to continue with it. Her pregnancy was not easy and very early on, doctors advised her against stress. Both Vishal and Ritu took a conscious decision that Ritu would take a break from her career.

Ritu was in the sixth month of her pregnancy. She was happy that Vishal had come in early and looked forward to spending time with him. Vishal changed his clothes and poured himself a drink, which alarmed Ritu. She was not against Vishal drinking, but Vishal was a social drinker and a rare drinker. He loved his beer on a hot Sunday afternoon, but she had never seen him have a drink at night. Even at parties, he would nurse one drink for a couple of hours, just to ensure that the host was not offended.

"What's the matter Vishal?"

"What?"

"Why are you having a drink?"

"The whisky will evaporate, if someone doesn't drink it."

Ritu did not respond but looked at him quizzically.

"Can't I have a drink once in six months?"

"In the past seven years, I have never seen you have a whisky alone, in the evening. What's the story?"

"Hey Ritu, what do you think I used to do in the evenings, when you were in Mumbai and I was in Delhi? How do you think I got over my loneliness?"

"Vishal, you cannot lie. So don't try that with me. What's the problem?"

"You caught me there Ritu. Let me tell you the entire story."

*****

After graduating with an MBA, Vishal joined an insurance company as their sales manager. Even though he joined as a manager, his job was to sell insurance. He had graduated with a specialization in Marketing but unfortunately, he was one amongst the last group of students to get placed from campus. He did not want to get into sales. However, at the back of his mind, he knew that he could not leave campus without a job as he had to settle down with Ritu. As he had no other option, he accepted the sales job.

To his surprise, he took to sales like a fish to water. He had a charming personality and was measured in his approach. The same qualities, which had led Ritu to fall in love with him in two months, were an asset in sales. His customers liked him, he was straight forward, honest and even had the guts to walk away from a sale, if the product was not right for the customer. This approach meant that he had a bad first three months, but it paid off. Customers from whom he had walked away actually called him to ask if he had any other product which suited them. He developed a huge trust with his customer base and that helped him sell his insurance products. As a principle, he never did a wrong sale, just to meet targets. In an industry famous for mis-selling, there was not one customer complaint against Vishal. He could sell big tickets, sell throughout the year, sell multiple products and so, gradually, he proceeded to top the charts.

Over a period of time, he got promotions on a fast track and today he was head of sales for the Northern Region.

He would frequently get pulled in to deliver training sessions on selling skills and was well respected by everybody in the organisation.

Three years ago he was called into a meeting by Sanjay, the Director of Sales, and Sudha, the Managing Director.

"Vishal, we want you to work on a concept that will disrupt the industry." Saying this Sanjay and Sudha gave him a one line brief. He understood the concept and immediately wrote a two page document on the same. He was hugely excited and understood the potential of the product, and realised that it would be a game changer.

However there was one constraint. There was no budget to develop this product. Even Vishal did not know how much it would cost. They were venturing into uncharted territory, Vishal did not even know whom to contact, and who would be these vendors. He also did not have resources, to work on the same. A combination of the above factors and year- end sales targets ensured that no work had been done on the same for nearly four months. In April, Sanjay and Sudha called him and asked him about progress on the project, and he had no answer.

The same evening, Sanjay took him out for a drink.

"Look Vishal, if anybody in the organisation can execute the project, it is you. Sudha herself said this, and has high expectations from you. Also it is Sudha's pet project. She is looking at you to take it to completion. You tell me what support you want and I will try to help you, but you have to lead it. We have no choice buddy. Also if we successfully achieve this, you will be in a different league"

Sanjay had played on Vishal's ego. Vishal now knew that he had no choice. He built on the concept paper he had written earlier, and with the help of a few handpicked colleagues, blessings from Sudha and funds from overseas partners, he started working on the same.

*****

"Ritu, you are aware, that we are working on an innovative product, which will take the market by storm. If implemented, it could stop mis-selling, or it could collect evidence that the customer had understood the product while buying it. You know that we have been working on it for two years now. We have done a pilot implementation, and unfortunately, it hasn't had the response we thought it would have."

"Since when are you concerned about failure Vishal? This is not the Vishal, I married! Have you become a coward?"

"Ritu, you know me very well. I am not afraid of failure, nor have I become a coward. I know exactly why the product has failed. Let me explain."

"Two years ago, when we started, we started developing the product on a computer based platform. That was a time, when Smart Phones weren't around and Tablet PCs had just started coming in. Six months into the project, we saw a smart-phone boom. I suddenly realised that we are working on the wrong platform. I proposed that we also develop an application for the product."

"Oh yes, I remember that. And I think you were shot down right? Today when Myntra.com has shut down its website, and has moved completely to an application platform, Flipkart and Make my Trip are launching app only sales, I realise your genius."

"Arjuna also was a genius, but he could not prevent Draupadi's disrobing."

"Is it the whisky speaking, or is it you?"

"Drinking is an adventure sport Ritu, and you know I don't like any sport where I am not in control. Even while I drink, I am in complete control."

"Arjuna is not your favourite character, how come you are mentioning him? Are you comparing yourself to Arjuna?"

"See, Arjuna may not be my favourite character, but I have respect for his talent and skills. While all the Pandavas were brilliant and talented, Arjuna was a huge asset for the Pandavas. My view is that the Pandavas had the confidence to get into conflict only on the basis of three people: Krishna's intelligence, Bheema's strength and Arjuna's skill. I am Arjuna in the current project. If I say this in office, I may be called arrogant, but I can mention this to you."

"Over the years Vishal, I have respected you for your conviction in yourself, your thoughts and your ideas. I recognise your genius and agree that you are Arjuna. I detect a sense of dejection in what you say. What are you trying to hint at when you say Arjuna could not stop Draupadi's disrobing?"

"Forget it. In the company of whisky, anything I say will be risky."

"*Topic hi risky hain Vishal.* Let's hear your analysis of what happened."

"Duryodhana invited Yudhishthir to a game of dice. Yudhishthir was a compulsive gambler as well as an expert and hence could not refuse the invitation. Shakuni, Duryodhana's maternal uncle played the game on behalf of the Kauravas. Initially the bets were small and Yudhishthir won quite a few of them. This is a classic casino trap. Even in casinos they let you win with small stakes and once you feel you are confident and on a roll, they invite you to play on tables with higher stakes. The same thing happened with Yudhishthir. As Shakuni started losing, he started increasing the stakes. It was a classic case of losing the battle to win the war."

"You mean to say, Shakuni deliberately lost? What if Yudhishthir had walked away with minor gains?"

"Very good point Ritu. Greed is an inherent part of human nature. Remember that when one is on a roll, they would like to make the most of it. It is said that the dice were loaded and Shakuni knew how to roll them. I personally don't believe that the dice were loaded, I actually think that Shakuni was highly skilled. See gambling is a game of skill, luck, as well as mind. Actually it is more mind and skill than luck. Yudhishthir, lost out to the mind and the skill. Shakuni was skilled enough to ensure that he did not win or lose always. He ensured that the results matched up to the probabilities."

"Vishal, now I am scared. You know so much about gambling."

"That is why I stay away from playing cards during Diwali. I have had my share of gambling losses which have taught me huge lessons."

"You used to gamble?"

"I lost a princely sum of twenty rupees, way back in college, but those seven days were enough to teach me a lot about gambling. So coming back to Yudhishthir and Shakuni. Even when the stakes were raised, Shakuni lost enough bets to make everybody believe that the game was fair. However at some point in time, the stakes became so high, that Yudhishthir gambled away his kingdom."

"Did he not realise at that time to back off and go away?"

"Actually he wanted to, but Shakuni offered to play another round with him. If Yudhishthir won, he would get back his entire kingdom."

"Is that when he put Draupadi at stake?"

"Yudhishthir said that he did not have anything to put at stake. The Kauravas then said that he could put himself and his brothers at stake. Anybody could have seen through the Kaurava cunning at that time. Two thought processes mattered at this point. One, without the kingdom, which they had painstakingly built, the Pandavas would be confined to a life of hardship and would have to live as hermits. This would be unfair to his brothers, his wife and his mother. He also believed in his dice throwing skills and the payoff was too huge. If he won, he could get his kingdom back and leave an honourable man."

"If anybody could see through the Kaurava cunning, was Yudhishthir blind?"

"Yudhishthir was not blind, but his mind was camouflaged by the gambler's syndrome. The problem with gambling is that no gambler wants to leave as a lost man. There is always the temptation to play an additional hand, to reduce the losses. Yudhishthir believed that he could win back his kingdom. He did not realise that Shakuni was playing him and not the game of dice."

"Amazing analysis Vishal, I always knew you are a genius and your analysis of gambling is a revelation. But interestingly, you are still avoiding the discussion."

"What discussion Ritu?"

"What is the connection to your project?"

"Arjuna's protests to Yudhishthir fell on deaf ears. Similarly my protests are also not being entertained."

"What are you protesting about Vishal?"

"The project that we are working on, has progressed slowly. We have completed 60% of the project and it is not successful. We are working on a computer based platform. All along I have been having discussions about moving to an application for Android and IOS platforms. Every time I say that, I am pushed back and told, 'let us finish the computer based platform first'."

"Isn't that the right thing to do Vishal?"

"Ritu, depends on the point of view. We Indians are extremely brilliant and even clairvoyant, but we don't count our blessings. I am not talking about being grateful to God or whatever. Do you know the single biggest contribution of politicians and our parents to our success?"

"This is definitely the whisky speaking."

"Maybe Ritu, but alcohol brings out the truth which can also be philosophical. Answer my question."

"I would rather let the whisky speak." Ritu had never seen Vishal in this mood before. She knew what would follow would be pearls of wisdom. She wanted to record this conversation, not to rib Vishal later when he would be sober, but to capture the thoughts. After all there is an old saying, 'Golden words are never repeated.' Today the petite Ritu, six months pregnant, weighed 60 kilograms. She was comfortably perched on the sofa and her movements had become slow. The mobile was far away and she did not want to disturb the trance Vishal was in.

"Our parents grew up in a very difficult environment. Not that they did not have two square meals to eat, but they definitely compromised on their pleasures to ensure that they gave us a great education. About the politicians, I know a lot of so called 'education barons' made money from education, but they made facilities available to us. Both of them realised the importance of education and have contributed to our success. Did you read in today's newspaper, that two brothers from a village in UP whose father is a daily wage earner, have secured admission into IIT? I think their father is a hero, and the family believes that the future of the children lies in education."

"Brilliant Vishal, but I think the whisky is slipping from one glass to another. I mean, we were talking about your project, Yudhishthir, and suddenly you want to thank your parents and politicians. What's the connection?"

"There is a connection. If our parents and politicians have been clairvoyant enough to understand the impact of education, even we need to look into crystal balls. We need to look into the future and see what will work. I think creating the project on a computer based platform is outdated. It is like creating a bullock cart in the jet age."

"Remember Vishal, India is a country where bullock carts co-exist with jet planes."

"Agreed, but ultimately where will the demand be high? For medium to high-end cars or bullock carts? Bullock carts may come back, not as a mode of transport, but as a rustic tourism experience. Today I actually told Sanjay to scrap the entire project and start afresh on the applications for Android or IOS."

"You are crazy. You actually said this to Sanjay? Since when have you started drinking in the afternoon?" Ritu asked.

Now it was Vishal's turn to get startled.

"I mean to say, for you to do what you did, you either need to be mad or high. I can't understand Vishal, it's your pet project and you are saying scrap it. It is like aborting a baby extremely late. It can be dangerous to the mother."

Ritu realised what she had blurted out and froze. Her statement was ironical, given that she herself was six months pregnant.

"I have no intention of aborting my baby dear." Vishal moved closer to her and took her in his arms. Two soulmates communicated to each other through a long silence. Vishal helped Ritu to the washroom, where she washed away her tears. They then proceeded to the dining table, laid out the food and both of them quietly started eating.

"Looks like there was an overdose of *khus khus* (poppy seeds) in the chicken this morning. Or you have completely lost it." Ritu broke the silence. Her comment on abortion had punctuated the conversation. She wanted to continue, wanted to understand Vishal's thought process in recommending scrapping of the project.

"I am not insane Ritu. I actually have been plagued by this thought for nearly two months. It was a very difficult conclusion to arrive at, but after giving it a lot of thought I am convinced it is the right decision."

"You will be wondering why I am saying this. Given the amount of money that has been put into this, scrapping the project will actually mean flushing the entire investment down the drain. But look at it dispassionately. The product is not yet complete, and completion will mean putting more money behind a project which is a loser."

"Vishal, I am amazed by your thought process, what was the reaction?"

"I have been shouted out. The arguments are exactly like a gambler. For a gambler to go back home after losing a substantial sum is openly accepting disgrace. You need a huge heart to accept your losses and mistakes, and go home. The people in the office are concerned about how to break the news to the stakeholders. How do we accept, that we are on a project which is now not looking good? There are also concerns about whether it is right to abandon it half way. Will they be branded as losers?"

"Come to think about it, the arguments are solid. What if you are wrong and the product proves to be a winner?"

"Yudhishthir thought in exactly the same fashion. What if he plays the last gamble and he wins? However in this case, the circumstantial evidence is damning. The world is moving towards applications. You have e-wallets and payment apps. RBI has granted licenses to Payment Banks. It might take ten years, but credit cards could also be history. You don't even have to look in the crystal balls. You just have to open your eyes. Actually it is a no brainer and a much simpler decision."

"I will tell you where the problem is Vishal. It is extremely difficult to let go. You will agree that your journey over the last two years has been exciting. All of you have handled it like your baby. You guys have put your own creativity, created it without any reference point. Even God replicates genes of parents in its creation. This is why it is difficult to discard it. Think, why do we have so many photographs, clippings, cards etc. stored in the attic and we don't discard them? Because there are memories attached to the same. Remember it is extremely difficult to let go and change."

"Do you think I have no emotional attachment to the project? It has completely been conceived by me. If I can give it up, anybody can."

"People are also afraid of failure Vishal. Not everyone is like you."

"If they were afraid of failure, they shouldn't have got into this in the first place. When we started we had no clue what we were getting into. It was innovation in its purest sense. Even geniuses don't get innovation right the first time. 'Do it Right the First Time', doesn't apply to innovation. It applies only when we know what we want as an end product. Innovation is a journey not a destination. Somewhere along the journey you get a light-bulb moment when you realise and understand what you are seeking to achieve. But the entire process is important. Here, when we have the light-bulb, people aren't willing to accept it."

"You are right Vishal. Innovators need a different DNA, and you have it. However, if you guys drop the project, how will it reflect in your appraisals?"

Ritu's words hit him in the solar plexus. He had picked up the whisky glass to put it to his lips but he froze midway and his hand started shaking. He put the glass down on the table and walked away. He paced the drawing room three times, came back and knelt and bowed to Ritu.

"Madam you are a genius."

He had realised the importance of the beautiful, performance appraisal system. Accepting that they have failed is giving management a rod to beat them with.

"Vishal, people are concerned about their ratings, increments, bonuses. Come to think of it, 80% of the people would rather be doing something else, if it were not for the money."

Suddenly a thought entered Vishal's mind and he laughed. "Should people work for the benefit of the organisation, or for a good performance appraisal? It is ironical, that in this case, if we pull the plug, and discard the project, which could actually be beneficial for the organisation, we will be pulled down in our performance appraisals. I agree, it takes guts to take such a decision, which, given the current circumstances, is the right thing to do. Nobody will reward us for the courage we have displayed in taking this decision. We will actually lose out on increments, bonuses etc. On the other hand, if we continue with the project, which may result in putting more money down the drain, we will be rewarded in our appraisals. It is like cheering Yudhishthir to play another game, and reprimanding him, when he backs out. I think I need another drink to digest this."

With this he got up to refill his whisky glass. Ritu was amazed at Vishal's take on the performance appraisal system. If this is how his thought process worked after a couple of drinks, he was wasting his talent. He just wasn't drinking frequently enough.

"So what do you plan to do?"

"What can I do? Like Arjuna, I have raised the objection, but Yudhishthir does not listen."

"Looks like history will repeat itself. Draupadi will again be disrobed."

"Tell me Ritu, what do I do?" The pain and helplessness in his voice was evident. Vishal had been extremely passionate about the project for the last two years, but now he didn't believe in it anymore. He displayed the same conviction that he always had and she was sure he was right. She also knew that if Vishal continued to work in this environment, he would be a mental wreck. For the first time, she had seen him pour a third drink.

Geniuses have two problems. One, they are a few years ahead of their time in thinking, and second, others don't easily understand them. Their energy, if not used or channelled properly, can destroy themselves. They have a self-destruct button which is inches away from their finger. She had to get him out of this mess... for him, for herself and for their unborn child. She had an idea... the conversation had to be taken to its logical conclusion.

"So what led up to Draupadi's disrobing??"

"Yudhishthir staked his brothers one by one. When he had lost them all, he finally staked his wife. He lost her too. All of this was taking place right in the middle of the court with all the elders present. Draupadi was menstruating at that time, and hence was not present in the court and was in her chamber. A summons was sent to Draupadi asking her to come to the court. When Draupadi was informed of the proceedings of the game of dice, the result, and in turn her summons, she sent the messenger back with a question. Did Yudhishthir stake her before losing himself or after that? If Yudhishthir had lost himself first, did he have a right to stake her?"

"Brilliant woman I must say."

"Yes. Great logical question by Draupadi. This however angered Duryodhana, who had a grudge against her. During the coronation of Yudhisthir in Indraprastha, the Kauravas were also invited. The grand palace was built by Maya the architect of the gods. It was a great construction full of illusion. What looked like a door was actually a wall. What seemed to be a pond was actually land. Duryodhana, while walking, was deceived by one of the illusions and fell into a pond. Draupadi, who was watching with her friends laughed and said aloud, 'Blind son of blind parents'. Duryodhana's father Dhritarashtra, the king of the Kauravas was born blind. When Gandhari, his wife learnt that she was marrying a blind king, she tied a scarf permanently over her eyes and voluntarily accepted blindness for life. Draupadi's insult was permanently entrenched in his mind.

Draupadi's refusal to come to court, along with her questioning of the wager and Duryodhana's insult, combined to send Duryodhana into a rage. Duryodhana instructed Dushasana his brother to get Draupadi to the court, whatever her current state. If she refused to come willingly, he was ordered to drag her to court."

"How inhuman. It was completely wrong on the part of Duryodhana to give out these instructions."

"Ritu, when one is angry, reason is absent. A lot of times you regret everything you say in anger. History paints Duryodhana as the villain. I don't say that what he did was right. However if we do a root cause analysis, we'll find that the situation would not have arisen if Yudhishthir had not put her up for stake. If I compare this to my project, Yudhishthir is staking his brothers one by one, and maybe even Draupadi. I can see it happening. Too much money is being used to flog a dead horse."

"Why don't you escalate?"

"What do I escalate Ritu? It is not a case of harassment, fraud or an improper conduct case that I can bring to the notice of say HR or the global partners. Everybody's intentions are genuine and they believe they are right. Ultimately this is just my opinion, I may be wrong, though I am sure I am right in this case. We will be wise only in hindsight."

"Why did the elders like Bhishma and Dhritarashtra, who were present, not stop Draupadi's disrobing?"

"I don't know but I can only speculate. Dhritarashtra may have been blinded by love for his son. My reading of the Mahabharata says that Bhishma had a soft corner for the Pandavas, however he followed his Dharma (duty). He had sworn that he would not be king, and would be loyal to the throne. Duryodhana was the king, and my guess is that even though Bhishma did not like it, he did not protest out of loyalty to the king. Also no law was broken, as Draupadi was being disrobed after she became the slave of Kauravas. Legally they were right, but morally they were wrong."

"So you are going to be Bhishma and be a witness to Draupadi's disrobing?"

"Do I have a choice?"

"You said Bhishma followed Dharma. I disagree. No concept of Dharma will allow a woman to be disrobed in public. Bhishma followed Rajdharma – he was loyal and did not speak out against Duryodhana. There is a difference between the two. Killing a human being is against Dharma while killing an opponent in war is Rajdharma. There are exceptional circumstances, where one has to abandon the path of Rajdharma and stick true to one's beliefs, values, conscience and follow the path of Dharma."

"So, you say I should tell Sudha my views? What happens to my relationships with Sanjay and the other colleagues who are on the project?"

"Since when have you been afraid of speaking the truth Vishal? If you were Bhishma during the Draupadi disrobing, would you have kept quiet?"

"Firstly I am not Bhishma, and secondly I may be wrong."

"You are avoiding the question."

"It is not so easy Ritu. By speaking out I will burn a lot of bridges. Also there are a few people who might lose their jobs. I will be responsible for that."

"Are you afraid that you will lose your job?"

This question startled Vishal. Ritu had brought out his worst fears on the table. The thought had never crossed his mind, but now it did. With the baby's birth being three months away, was it a risk worth taking? He went to pour himself another drink.

"Vishal, we spend a lot of time in our corporate lives trying to satisfy everybody, and arriving at a 'compromise solution'. I know that they say that one should not burn bridges in corporate life. But there is a difference between standing up to your convictions and burning bridges. A lot of times, people in the organisation cannot distinguish between dissent and politics. The dividing line is very thin. Where does your integrity lie? Is it with the company, or with your managers? By trying to protect your relationship with your managers, you will actually be hurting the company, which in turn hurts these managers also. About the people who might lose their jobs, are they married to the company for life? They are there in the first place because they have skills that you need. I am sure they will find jobs. More importantly, will you be able to work on a product which you don't believe in?"

Vishal looked at Ritu and smiled. "Time to go to bed dear." He knew what to do. He got up and poured the freshly filled glass of whisky down the drain.

He would not be the silent Bhishma. He had never worked on projects he had not believed in. If it meant walking out on Duryodhana, so be it. He would protest against Draupadi's disrobing. He would search for a different kingdom, or set one up himself.

KARNA'S REPUTATION

"You don't care about Vivaan. Your work is more important. I don't think I am anything more than a corporate widow."

Garima picked up their three year old child, slammed the bedroom door and locked it from inside. Kunal had no answer to this argument and resigned himself to spending the night on the sofa.

Kunal was an Associate in one of the major accounting firms in the country. Working with a key accounting firm was like being trapped in a golden cage. The pay was good, work was good and the facilities at the clients' offices were even better. As consultants they were pampered. However the workload was tremendous. Ten hour work days were the minimum, and twelve was the norm. There were days when Kunal would return home at two a.m. only to leave home at seven. Sometimes he felt like a paying guest in his own home, as he went there only to sleep and change clothes. The firm had its own horror stories. One of the partners was rumoured to have seen his new-born baby only after three days, because he was in the office for more than 48 hours at a stretch.

Garima's latest outburst was an outcome of the upcoming Parent Teachers Meeting in school. It was scheduled for

Thursday morning at eleven. There was no way Kunal would be able to make it for the same. After all, Thursday was when he had a lunch invitation with a very Senior Partner in the firm. An Associate met Partners only for a few minutes during the time of finalisation of the report, and here Kunal had a lunch invitation with her. More importantly, he had never worked with her and she had invited him for lunch. Kunal was both eager and anxious about this meeting.

Kunal was bright and extremely hardworking. Due to his brilliance, he could do his assigned work in half the time that others required to complete the same. He kept on looking out for assignments where he could help. He had the ability to easily switch from one assignment to another and his raw analysis of the clients' problems was amazing. He had slowly gained a reputation for his simple, out of the box solutions and clarity of thought. He became very sought after, and worked on multiple projects simultaneously. He was someone who never said no to an assignment.

This habit had been inculcated in him by his mentor, Rajesh. Rajesh was a complete maverick. Extremely brilliant, he never followed the conventional path in his thoughts and career. After qualifying as an accountant, he had landed a job in the largest FMCG multinational in the world at that time. Out of 27 candidates interviewed, he was the only one selected. He was doing extremely well, but against all conventional wisdom resigned within six months. His contention was that there was no growth in his job. His parents were at their wits end wondering, how could one discount growth prospects in six months? He then prepared a taxation software and sold it to various businesses. He became an expert in Microsoft Excel and Word and then joined a publishing company, advising them on technicalities on Microsoft Word. He was a classic blend of traditionalism and modernity. He was extremely well read in the epics, with Mahabharata being his favourite. He said that Mahabharata was so complex, that every situation in human life, will have a parallel in the Mahabharata.

Currently Rajesh spent his time teaching and consulting. Kunal met him when he was undergoing coaching for the Chartered Accountancy exam. Kunal himself was extremely bright, confident and ahead of the rest of his class. Rajesh spotted his confidence, and one day on the way back from class offered Kunal a lift. Among various things, Rajesh had told Kunal, "The dividing line between self confidence and arrogance, is extremely thin. There is a danger of falling over to the other side." At that time, Kunal did not understand this statement. He decided to select Rajesh as his mentor. After qualifying successfully as a Chartered Accountant, he had gone to Rajesh's house to seek his blessings.

"In the first five years of your career, you need to be a sponge and absorb everything that is thrown at you. You should never say no, because those are the formative years.

Yashaswi bhava (May you be successful)" was Rajesh's advice to him.

*****

There are two kinds of people in every organisation. One set of people talk about what they are doing, and advertise it openly to seniors. They never miss an opportunity to mingle with seniors in the elevator, or on a smoke break. They ensure that they make their presence felt; this helps them during year end evaluations. Fair or unfair is a separate issue, but the fact is this strategy works. If you are good and can also 'market' yourself that is a deadly combination.

Then there is the second set of people, the silent workers. Their work speaks for them. Recognition may take a bit longer, but once it does, the evidence and weight it carries is irrefutable. Every organisation has these diamonds, but the problem is they are hidden. They don't believe in talking about their work. Not that they can't talk. If given an opportunity, they can come up with pearls of wisdom. Bright ideas, innovative solutions and great execution skills come out of here. Kunal belonged to this category of people.

Three weeks ago, Kunal had a heated discussion with Mukesh in the elevator about the impact of new Indian Accounting Standards and the convergence with IFRS. Little did he know, Vidya was in the elevator with them.

Vidya was a senior partner in the firm. With twenty years' experience in the firm, she was favourite to take over the leadership of the firm. She was extremely well recognised in the business world, was a leading expert, and frequently quoted in the media. Vidya's ears perked up when she heard somebody talking about Accounting Standards. She recognised Kunal from the induction a few years ago as he had made her distinctly uncomfortable at that time.

*****

"Madam, in the Satyam case, do you think the auditors were negligent, or were part of the conspiracy?" Kunal was first off the blocks to ask. He did not want to lose the opportunity to pick a senior partner's brain during the induction

"Can you please introduce yourself?" Vidya was buying time.

"I am Kunal Batra."

"And why do you think that auditors were part of the conspiracy?" Vidya tried to dodge the uncomfortable question.

"How can a few thousand crores of fixed deposits not exist? Especially when the biggest auditing firms talk about quality and due diligence and documentation, should they not have insisted on verifying the receipts before signing off on the audit? After all the amounts are material."

(Ramalinga Raju the chairman of Satyam had admitted in a press conference that the balance sheet had a hole of a few thousand crores and that was the result of fixed deposits which did not exist. Subsequently Raju was jailed for fraud.)

"Well I do not have any inside information and cannot comment on the culpability or otherwise of a fellow professional." Vidya had sidestepped the question; but Kunal had created an impression. She had made a mental note to follow his progress, but caught in the usual truckload of work she had forgotten about it.

*****

The day she overheard his argument in the elevator, she remembered her earlier resolve. She checked on his progress through the years. She had been impressed at the induction and she was impressed with what she had heard. She decided that she would take Kunal under her wings and scheduled a lunch meeting with him. She had to cancel a few appointments, but realised that it was worth it. After all one rarely finds a diamond in a gold mine.

Kunal's son had joined play school three months ago and this was his first parent teachers meeting (PTM). He had decided to take leave on the day of the PTM and take

Garima and Vivaan for an outing. He had even mentioned this to Garima and she was overjoyed.

But this morning he received a phone call from Lisa, Vidya's Executive Assistant. She informed Kunal that Vidya wanted to meet Kunal for lunch on Thursday, at noon at the Taj President. Kunal was stumped.

"Lisa, are you sure you are speaking to the right person?"

"You are Kunal Batra?"

"Yes."

"Then you are to meet her for lunch. What's your preference, Thai or Italian?"

"Whatever Vidya prefers."

Ok. So meet her at the Trattoria and don't be late or back out as Vidya has cancelled two client meetings to have lunch with you."

Her words hit Kunal forcefully and he could not refuse. He was sure it was not a disciplinary issue, as he did not remember doing anything wrong. Moreover, you don't do disciplinary hearings over lunch at the Taj President!

However he was also intrigued by the fact that a senior partner with whom he had never interacted had invited him for lunch. When he came back to Mother Earth, he realised that the date clashed with his son's first PTM and he had committed to Garima to take her out for lunch.

After reaching home, when he broke the news to his wife, tempers flew. Kunal had no answer because Garima had every right to be angry.

Thursday morning, when he came out of the shower, he found his clothes laid out. This was a huge surprise. In a lot of Indian households, the dutiful wife would lay out clothes for the husband to wear to office. A lot of wives found joy in doing this. However in the case of Kunal and Garima the situation was different. Kunal was independent and would only ask Garima for an opinion and would select his own clothes for the day, unless he was running late, when he would request Garima to lay them down. Today, without any request Garima had laid down the clothes. Also there was a rectangular box on the bed, which was gift wrapped and had a card which mentioned "Best of luck to a new beginning." Kunal opened the box to find a brand new tie. Blue was his favourite colour and Kunal loved it.

Men really can't understand women. For the past three days, since he had broken the news about the meeting, he had been receiving the 'silent treatment' and sleeping on the sofa at nights. And then this?

Well, Garima was angry with Kunal, but she also realised how important this meeting was for him. She understood the rationale behind Kunal's decision, but a woman's anger takes time to ebb. Spouses may be angry with their husbands but they always have his best interests in mind.

Kunal took Garima in his arms and started feeling guilty. He did not know what to say. Garima smiled at him and said, "We can go out some other time. And, after all, a PTM for a play school is not so important."

A huge load off his head, Kunal drove to Taj President. He entered Trattoria and saw her seated at the table. She was elegantly dressed in a pastel pink saree and was wearing a pearl necklace. With glasses on, she was reading up some stuff on her smart phone. Kunal walked to the table and greeted her

"Good afternoon madam."

"Kunal, what a pleasure to meet you. Please sit."

"It's such an honour to have lunch with you Madam."

"Please call me Vidya. Do you like prawns?"

"Yes Vidya."

"You should try the Cocktail Gamberi here. It is very good….So why do you think I have called you?"

"I have no clue. Please tell me."

"Firstly you are among the few people who have made me uncomfortable. Remember the induction?"

Kunal suddenly went back in time. He remembered his question and how Vidya had nicely avoided answering it. All his peers in the induction had told him, that by asking this question, he had committed professional suicide.

Even when he had joined, his manager questioned him about the incident. He was wondering whether he had made a mistake. He went and narrated the incident to Rajesh. "*Karmanye wadhika raste... Ma Faleshu Kadachan.*" (Do your duty and do not worry about the consequences.) Rajesh recited from the Gita. (The Gita is the holy book of the Hindus. At the beginning of the war, Arjuna was reluctant to fight as his opponents were his cousins and uncles. At that time, Krishna had recited the Gita and reminded Arjuna of his duty and convinced him to fight the war.)

"Sir, I don't understand Sanskrit," replied Kunal. Rajesh smiled and reminded him of their first meeting. "I had told you that the dividing line between confidence and arrogance is very thin. Whether an action of yours is self-confidence or arrogance depends upon perception. Your peers and seniors, who are less talented than you, will perceive your thoughts as arrogance, while you think it is confidence. What you are experiencing is exactly this. While you should do your duty, please be aware of this and be careful in what you say."

His thoughts were interrupted by the arrival of Cocktail Gamberi. He made a mental note to talk to Rajesh later in the day.

"This is delicious Vidya. Thanks for the recommendation. So am I going to pay today for making you uncomfortable five years ago?"

"I will pick up the tab today, but you need to repay the debt." Vidya decided to indulge in some banter.

"Can we not write it off Vidya?" Kunal decided to play the game. Vidya had converted an innocuous statement of his into a play of words.

"If we do that, we will have to reclassify you as an NPA – a non performing asset." Vidya replied with a smile.

"You got me there Vidya. Tell me what can I do for you?"

"Kunal you definitely made an impression on me during the induction. I had decided to keep watch on you, but due to work pressure it slipped out of my mind. And then a couple of weeks back, I heard your views on the Indian Accounting Standards and convergence with IFRS."

Kunal's soup spoon stopped midway between the soup bowl and his mouth. It went back into the bowl.

"How do you know my views?"

"You got to be careful young man. Last week I heard you talk passionately in the elevator. You were so passionate about the Accounting Standards; you didn't even notice the lady who was already in the elevator. I must say I was impressed by that five minute monologue. I then went and checked about your progress in the organisation. I must say that everybody has good things to say about you."

"Thank you for the compliments."

"I want you to do a small project for me. Will you have the time?"

"Vidya, I will give an arm and a leg to directly work with you. Your wish is my command."

After that they spent time discussing the details of the project. Kunal was extremely pleased at the way the meeting progressed. He immediately stepped out and called his mentor Rajesh and informed him of the development.

"I am extremely happy Kunal. This calls for a celebration. Let's meet for dinner, my treat."

"Thanks a lot sir, but there is a problem." And then he narrated the entire episode of his late nights and his fallout with Garima.

"No problems Kunal, I understand. It is nice that you have started thinking about your family. But I need to meet you. Let's meet next Friday for dinner, come home. Bring Garima and Vivaan along."

Kunal couldn't refuse. He was sure that Garima would not mind, she actually liked visiting Rajesh and his family.

On Friday evening Kunal, Garima and Vivaan reached Rajesh's house.

"Come Kunal let's go into the study and have a drink." Rajesh left the ladies and children and whisked Kunal away. After all, there was a purpose behind his invitation to Kunal.

"So Kunal how are you doing?'

"Excellent sir, doing some great work. And then I told you about the project with Vidya. Sir, she is an amazing lady and working with her is like working with a walking encyclopaedia. She has great knowledge and I am learning huge perspectives from her."

"I am so happy for you. So you are working on two projects at a time." Rajesh sensed an opening and entered

"No sir, at any given point of time, I am working on five projects."

"Looks like, the firm is making you work for your salary. Five projects together is just too great. How many projects do your peers work on?"

"Well, all of us are allotted one project at a time. I am also allotted one project plus there is Vidya's project. The others… I just keep on helping out people." Kunal did not realise that he was himself opening the door, inch by inch for Rajesh. The conversation was going exactly the way Rajesh wanted it to.

"Great Kunal. But do you get credit for the same?"

"It does not matter sir. I have been following your instructions. You told me to soak up whatever work comes my way. I am not doing it for credit, I am doing it for the learning experience."

"But should your seniors not know about your capabilities and what you are doing?"

"I am sure they know sir. Otherwise, why would Vidya pick me out of the blue for a special project?"

"I thought that was the result of your elevator conversation."

"It was, but she enquired about me and said she got good feedback. I am a firm believer that your work speaks for yourself and you get credit when it is due."

"Very good. The more I look at you, the more I see shades of Karna in you." Rajesh suddenly shifted the topic to the Mahabharata.

"Thank you for comparing me with Karna. But I am not even half as talented as he was.

"Kunal you are aware that Karna was born with Kawacha-Kundala, a body of armour and golden earrings. As long as he had these, he could not be killed."

"Well I knew that. But he was finally killed by Arjuna in war. So how did Arjuna manage to achieve that?"

"Karna was the son of Surya, the sun god. Every day he used to pray to the sun at sunrise and sunset. During sunset after his prayers, he used to conduct a donation camp. Whoever came to him never went away empty handed, and if it was in Karna's powers he would donate the same. Karna was also known as Daan Veer – the 'Charitable One'. He had an exemplary reputation for not turning anyone away empty-handed. "

"Wow that is an amazing quality."

"Should people be prisoners of their reputation?" Rajesh asked this out of the blue.

Rajesh would narrate an episode from the Mahabharata and then ask a seemingly unrelated question, which in fact would be related to the story. Despite knowing this, Kunal was startled.

"Your reputation is everything you have. If you are true to your reputation, it defines you as a person and defines your character. People can rely and depend on you." Kunal did not understand the meaning of Rajesh's question.

"Agreed Kunal. It takes a lifetime to develop a reputation, and just one aberration to destroy it. Reputations are built brick by brick and need to be protected. My question is what lengths will you go to, to protect your reputation?"

"Sir, this is overhead transmission. You are getting too philosophical and I am not able to understand a word of what you are saying."

"Ok… so here you go. How does one develop a reputation?"

"One creates a reputation by displaying consistent behaviour in a given situation."

"Let us assume that there is an upright non-corrupt official "A". I am sure that he generates a halo and reputation of not being corrupt. How does this reputation get created?"

"By doing the right thing and refusing bribes consistently when they are offered."

"Fantastic. Let's now say there is another official "B" who has exactly the opposite reputation. How will this have been created?"

"He would have compromised on his ethics repeatedly and word would have spread."

"Very good Kunal. Now if "B" receives a proposal which he does not agree with and wants to reject it, how easy will it be to do the same?"

"Very difficult, because people know that B compromises on his ethics and hence he will be repeatedly subject to this test. And of course anything that is arguable has a price."

"Exactly, slowly "B" is becoming a prisoner of his own reputation. Does it make sense Kunal?"

"Partly... it is still sinking in..."

I will give you another example. Do you remember M.F. Hussain? "

"The great painter?"

"Yes."

"What about him?"

"What else was he famous for other than his painting?"

"His muses?"

"Good one Kunal. But do you know that he was turned away from a reputed South Mumbai club because he arrived barefoot? "

"Ridiculous."

"Yes it is, but what is more ridiculous is that it made news. It was in the newspapers all around. Now Hussain developed a reputation that he walked around barefoot. And subsequently I am sure he would have made efforts to cultivate this reputation. Imagine moving around Mumbai barefoot in the monsoons. Even if he wanted to wear footwear, he could not, as he had a reputation to protect. In fact he had become a prisoner of his reputation."

"As usual sir, you are amazing. We have always heard about consistency in behaviour, creating your personal brand, creating a reputation for oneself but for the first time I am hearing about being a prisoner of one's reputation. How is it linked to Karna? If I know you well, you do not pull a thread out of the blue."

"So here is the rest of Karna's story. Arjuna was the son of Indra. And Indra was worried that if anybody could vanquish his son it was Karna. Karna could not be killed as long as he had his kavacha-kundala. So he took the guise of a poor Brahmin and approached Karna during his donation camp and asked for his Kavacha-kundala."

"That is unfair!" exclaimed Kunal.

"Everything is fair in love and war Kunal. The interesting part is that Surya, the Sun God, who was Karna's father, appeared in his dreams and told him that Lord Indra in the guise of a Brahmin would approach him and ask him for his Kavacha-kundala."

"What? So Karna knew of the conspiracy! So did he give them?"

"Karna was in a dilemma. He had already been cursed twice and he did not want another curse from a dissatisfied Brahmin. He also had a reputation of not turning away anyone empty handed. He had become a prisoner of his reputation. He gave away his Kavacha-kundala without flinching, which made him vulnerable."

"Wow, what selflessness."

"If you are Karna, would you give away your Kavach-kundala today?"

"No way sir. That's my biggest protective cover. Giving it away will leave me vulnerable."

"Are you slowly becoming the *daanveer* Karna of your office?" Rajesh slipped one in innocuously.

Kunal was left gaping at Rajesh when he heard this statement. It was as if he had a lightbulb moment. He realised what Rajesh was saying, but could not believe he had said it.

"What do you mean sir?"

"You work on five projects at a time, help everybody, and never say no to work; are you developing a reputation for being 'Mr. Dependable'?"

"What's wrong in that sir?" Kunal knew what Rajesh was implying. He wanted to digest it, and wanted a greater explanation for the same.

"Nothing wrong Kunal. You are creating a great reputation for yourself. But will this reputation kill you?"

"How can it kill me sir?" He just wanted Rajesh to spell out the answer for him.

"Firstly, if you help others with their assignments who will benefit?"

"It doesn't matter if they benefit, get credit or even get promoted. Nobody can take away what is mine."

"What are your current working hours?"

"How is that linked here sir?"

"Answer my question."

"I leave home at 8 a.m. and by the time I am home, it is generally 9 p.m."

"How many times do you have dinner with your son?"

"Maybe twice a week."

"Which is Saturday and Sunday." Rajesh quipped.

Kunal did not reply. He just looked down, Rajesh had hit the nail on the head.

"It is not that I don't want to have dinner with Vivaan sir, but you know work pressures."

"Kunal, stop fooling yourself. The work pressures are created by you. If you are working on five projects at a time, out of which three belong to others, where is the pressure?"

"Sir, I can finish my work and easily leave by six at least three times a week. But then everybody is in office till at least eight. It will look odd if I leave early. It is not only about working hard, it is also about being seen as hard-working."

"Ah... the classic showcase trap. See, you are getting trapped in your own reputation of being a hard worker. How many times have you said no to any additional work?"

"Never sir. But isn't that what you advised me? Soak up all the work in the formative years."

"I did that Kunal, but are you developing a reputation for accepting everything that is thrown at you? One of the important qualities is the ability to say no. It can be about the work you don't want to do, or about not having adequate bandwidth. In case you get work thrown at you, and don't have bandwidth to execute, do you think you will do justice to it? What will happen to quality?"

"Obviously quality could suffer."

"What if quality suffers, Kunal? Or worse if you slip up on timelines?"

"The damage will be huge sir."

"And who will be responsible for the damage?"

With this statement, Rajesh picked up Kunal's glass and refilled it. The silence in the room was ringing out loud.

"Will people forgive you for slip up in quality or timelines, just because you have too many assignments? I don't think so. You will be blamed for biting off more than you can chew."

"So what do I do sir?"

"Your points about cultivating a reputation are right. But pick and choose projects where you want to contribute. Maybe let go some of them, just to ensure people don't take you for granted. Like in war, always keep the opponent guessing. If you have spare time, spend it with Vivaan and Garima. You need to take a life view and not a simple career view. Play to win, and don't let your reputation make you vulnerable as it happened with Karna."

Kunal now knew why Rajesh had invited him for dinner. He wondered whether Garima had spoken to Rajesh. But he immediately dismissed the thought as he knew Garima would never do something like that. He realised he was fortunate to have Rajesh as a well-wisher, who could see the other side when things are seemingly going good and give warnings well in advance.

After all there is a price to pay for success… and Kunal wondered if success in itself was a paradox!

ABHIMANYU

"Yess!!!" Their strong cry of achievement pierced the silence at 12,000 feet. Ajay and Atul cried out loud, burst into high fives and hugged each other, feeling a great sense of achievement.

It had begun six months ago, when Ajay announced that he was going to visit Tungnath, which at 12,000 feet is the highest Shiva temple in the world. He was sure he wanted to go, and asked his friends to join him. It was an arduous journey involving multiple modes of transport from Mumbai where he lived; a flight to Delhi, an overnight train to Haridwar and then, a long 200 kilometres car trip on continuously winding roads, at the end of which was Dev Bhoomi, with vegetarian food and no alcohol. All of this to visit one temple? Religious tourism wasn't exactly everyone's cup of tea amongst Ajay's friends.

Atul had learnt surfing in Australia while visiting his elder sister who had settled down in Sydney after getting married. On a trip to the Gold Coast in Queensland, his brother-in-law had introduced him to the water sport. Since then he was hooked on to surfing.

The pursuit of Management Education took him to Manipal, in Karnataka. Manipal is a unique town-village. It has a population of around 50,000 out of which 30,000 is a floating population. It has a large number of educational institutions ranging from engineering and medical colleges to management institutes. The floating population is actually a microcosm of the entire country and comprises mostly of students.

When he reached Manipal, he found virgin beaches with crystal clear water and huge waves in the vicinity. After his term break, he carried his surf board. He took a few of his classmates surfing and they were hooked.

He suddenly realised the potential for a business idea. He opted out of placements and set up a surfing school on Malpe beach, which was 10 kms from Manipal. After all, if you enjoy what you do, you don't have to work a single day in your life. August being the time when surfing was not possible due to heavy rains, Atul had agreed to join Ajay on his Tungnath hike.

Ajay loved the natural beauty of Uttarakhand and wanted to test himself and his fitness. Three years ago he had taken his parents for the Char Dham trip. On the way, they had stopped at the little village of Chopta for breakfast. The natural beauty of the village mesmerised him. The horizon was dotted with snow clad peaks, turning orange with the rays of the rising sun. He could hear the silence of nature. Nanda Devi, Trishul Parbat and other peaks were staring at him like gods from the sky. Standing at the edge of the road and staring at beautiful green meadows below, Ajay felt simply overwhelmed and dwarfed by nature.

"*Saahab aapka paratha.*" (*Sir your paratha*) Ajay's thoughts were punctuated by these words from the Dhaba wala. When he turned around, he saw a small mountain adjoining the road with a temple on top. The valley was so beautiful that he had completely missed seeing the temple on his left.

"What temple is that?"

"That is Tungnath. The highest Shiva temple in the world and one of the Panch Kedars."

"What is Panch Kedar?" asked an ignorant Ajay. A hot paratha at 8,500 feet, with temperatures around 15 degrees Celsius punctuated by the warm sun is a great setting to listen to a story.

"The story is related to the Mahabharat. After the war, the Pandavas were told to seek forgiveness from Lord Shiva, as they were guilty of '*gotra hatya*', killing their brethren. So they went out in search of the Lord. Shiva thought that the Pandavas were guilty and hence to avoid them, he had taken the form of a bull. Once the Pandavas realised this, Bhima with his supernatural powers, grew to his full size and ordered all the cattle to pass between his legs. Shiva the bull started running in the other direction, as gods cannot and should not pass under the legs of humans. Once the bull was identified, the Pandavas ran behind it. When they caught it, the bull disintegrated and its parts fell in five different places; the face surfaced in the Pashupatinath temple in Nepal. Tungnath is the place where the 'bahu' (hands) were seen. You must have come from Kedarnath, where the hump is seen."

"You mean to say, that Kedarnath is also one of the Panch Kedars?"

"Of course, on the way you would have passed Ukhimath, which is the winter abode of the Panch Kedars. The replicas of all the Kedars are present in the temple at Ukhimath. Did you not see the same?"

He was suddenly ashamed of himself. Being a Vice President in one of the largest banks of the world, he was at the pinnacle of his success and believed he knew everything. He took pride in the fact that he would gather all facts before taking any decision. He had visited Kedarnath and did not know about the legend of Panch Kedar. He had stayed at Ukhimath and not visited the temple. As Ajay was agnostic, he was not a great fan of temples. After all India has a temple at every 100 metres. Even *'saat janam'*, seven lifetimes, are not adequate to visit all temples in India. But now he realised what he had missed. The story of Panch Kedar fascinated him, and here he had no understanding of India's mythology. He decided to go back and read up various mythological texts. And he promised himself that he would come back to Chopta and to Tungnath.

Over the next two years Tungnath stayed in the cache of his brain. One day in a party with his close friends, he announced he was visiting Tungnath. "I am going in August, anybody wants to come? Else I will go alone." Atul was the only person who decided to go with him.

Tungnath is the easiest of the five Panch Kedars. It is a small 4 km trek on a paved path. Ajay was forty, balding and putting on weight. He had put on ten kilos in the last one year. He knew the virtues of exercise, but could never get himself to begin the same. This was one area where he was an expert at procrastination. At the age of forty, after years of breathing pure, vehicle emission contaminated air in Mumbai, he wondered whether he could still do this simple trek. Ajay also wanted to test his fitness.

He had his share of vacations which he had enjoyed, but each of them was punctuated with conference calls from his office. But he knew that in the large hilly areas of Uttarakhand, mobile signals were extremely weak. He wanted to get away from everything for three days. Away from calls, away from office pressures; he wanted to be with himself and nature and maybe a few close friends to have fun with.

He was wondering what would happen if he was incommunicado for a week. When he had talked to his bosses, about his vacation plan and that he may not be accessible, the reactions were interesting. He was given an impression that without him the world would end. Not exactly the world, but surely the firm would close down.

He wondered whether the management expected him to respond to his emails on the blackberry in case he was hospitalised. He felt that asking for a week's leave, is like seeking permission to commit a crime. Two weeks leave is culpable homicide, and three weeks is like committing multiple gory crimes.

The accommodation he had chosen was deliberately a tent in a meadow with no electricity. He wanted to see, if the world could survive without him for three days. People go to temples to seek blessings and wishes. For Ajay, Tungnath was just an excuse to get away from everything. He was seeking answers, not from God but from himself. Tungnath was just a historical place, set amidst the beauty of nature, a perfect place for him to seek peace and isolation.

But the Lord has his own ideas. Little did he know that during this trip he would face one of his biggest career challenges, and discover the solution at the same time.

Exhausted, and with a sense of achievement, Ajay and Atul, went into the temple. Along with the priest, they were the only people in the temple. It was starkly different from the "famous" places of worship. It was an old structure with barely enough space for four people to sit down comfortably. The priest did a brief puja which lasted for 10 minutes. Ajay and Atul could not expect to spend even two minutes in any of the famous temples in India because there would be a huge crowd, people would push and the priests would egg them on to move ahead. But here was the highest Shiva temple in the world, a place of huge historical significance with no one inside it. The priest told them that this was also the place where Lord Vishnu offered penance and got his Sudarshan Chakra.

Suddenly two agnostic people wanted to spend more time in the temple. For maybe the first time in their lives they realised what it meant to spend time in the presence of God. They spent another 10 minutes, simply sitting with their eyes closed after the priest left.

Happy with their rendezvous with Lord Shiva, they left the temple. Soon, they were struck by hunger pangs. They entered a small shack and ordered lunch.

Sitting in the corner was a dishevelled, unshaven man in his late fifties, wearing saffron robes. He was staring continuously at Ajay. After some time, the stares made him uncomfortable.

"Kya baat hain baba, aise kyon dekh rahe ho?" (*What's the matter, why are you looking at me like that?*)

"Tum Abhimanyu ho." (*You are Abhimanyu.*)

"No baba, my name is Ajay and I have come from Mumbai."

"Tumhare zindagi mein bahut jald ek Abhimanu yog aane waala hain." (*Very soon you are going to get an Abhimanyu experience.*)

"Please take his words seriously. These people are gifted and have a connection with the occult. Whether you believe him or not, don't ridicule or make fun of him. Don't offend him, else he will curse you. He has seen something in your future." The shack owner whispered in Ajay's ear while serving lunch. He had seen these Bombay, Delhi types. They would make fun and ridicule the Babas who would get angry. These educated people who would climb Tungnath wearing shorts, carrying fancy cameras and drinking only mineral water, think that just because they earn good money, they can make fun of anybody.

Hearing this Ajay stiffened. He remembered his last visit to Chopta. He had promised himself that he would go back and read the various mythological texts. His promise was lost in the deluge of presentations, project reports, proposals, meetings and appraisals. He cursed himself for not reading up.

"Abhimanyu ki kahaani bataiye na baba." (*Please tell us Abhimanyu's story.*) Ajay requested with folded hands. They were tired and needed to rest. He decided that it was a good way to pay respect to the Baba.

"Abhimanyu is the son of Arjuna and Subhadra. Extremely brave and valiant, he died fighting singlehandedly against all the Kaurava *maharathis* (Great Warriors) in the battlefield."

"It was the thirteenth day of the Mahabharata war. Dronacharya was leading the Kaurava army and had employed the Chakravyuha formation. It was a seven-layered formation with each internal layer stronger than the earlier layer. The Kaurava army approached the battlefield in the shape of seven concentric circles with a small gap at the front. The gap would be used to ensnare and trap the enemy. Every time a soldier from the first circle would be killed, an adjacent soldier would step in and close the gap leaving just a narrow mouth for the enemy to enter. There were only two people in the Pandava camp who knew how to break this formation – Arjuna and his son Abhimanyu. Dronacharya had smartly engaged Arjuna in a different part of the battlefield. However, Abhimanyu's knowledge of Chakravyuh was incomplete.

Abhimanyu had learnt how to break into the Chakravyuh in his mother's womb. One evening, when Arjuna and a heavily pregnant Subhadra were enjoying moments of solitude and togetherness, Subhadra asked him about the Chakravyuh formation. Arjuna started describing the same. He talked about the formation, how to break it and enter it. Unfortunately by the time he started talking about how to exit the Chakravyuh, Subhadra was fast asleep. Hence Abhimanyu could not learn the technique of exiting from the Chakravyuh.

Yudhisthir realised on seeing the formation that this could be the end. The Pandava army was falling fast. At that time, Abhimanyu went to his uncle and said that he knew how to enter the Chakravyuh, but did not know how to exit. Yudhisthir told him to break the Chakravyuh and said that behind him, the Pandava army would enter and destroy the Chakravyuh from inside.

However that was not to be. Once Abhimanyu broke the Chakravyuh, Jayadratha stepped in and closed the gap. Nobody else from the Pandava army could enter and Abhimanyu was fighting the battle inside the Chakravyuh himself. He managed to break through and reach the core of the Chakravyuh, where he started battling the Kaurava *maharathis.* In the fierce battle they disarmed him. Finally he started battling using the wheel of his chariot as a shield. Alas, the rules of war were not followed and a disarmed Abhimanyu was killed."

"What a brave warrior! And a hugely fascinating story. Thank you Baba." He wanted to offer money to the Baba, but he decided to check with the shack owner.

"It is a good thing that you asked saaheb. *Baba ko paise nahin, khana khila do... Wo bhi namrata se poochke."* (Dont offer money to baba, ask him humbly if he will have lunch.)

Both Ajay and Atul quietly started walking back to the base, where the car was waiting. On the way back there was a flock of eagles flying. One eagle suddenly started descending and came very close to Ajay, then, it suddenly took vertical flight and went away. It was as if the eagle descended just to give Ajay a closer glimpse of itself. Ajay was mesmerised by the whole episode. Unfortunately, Atul had stopped to take a leak and he missed the sight.

"Atul, you won't believe what I just saw. The eagle mock landed, and soared suddenly. It was amazing, you just missed it"

"It's a sign." Atul said.

"What do you mean?"

"Do you know, whose vehicle is the eagle?"

"No... You tell me."

"It is the vehicle of Lord Vishnu. You came here to meet Lord Shiva, at the place where Vishnu did penance and obtained the Sudarshan Chakra. My friend, you have just been blessed by Lord Vishnu."

"Don't talk rubbish, Atul. You operate from the temple town of Udupi. Udupi is famous for the Sri Krishna temple and Krishna is an avatar of Vishnu. If anything the blessings are meant for you."

"Exactly my point Ajay. We have been seeing eagles hovering around since morning. The eagle picks a time when I am busy and gives you... only you ... a sighting? The hand of God is evident."

Ajay dismissed the topic and started the downward descent. On reaching down, his cell phone rang. For the last two days, no one could reach him. And suddenly, when he was about to step in the car, it rang. Ajay answered the call. It was his Director. After a few minutes, during which Ajay was only in the listening mode, the call broke. He got into the car. Atul was already asleep.

"*Camp chale sir?*" (*Shall we go to the camp?*) asked the driver.

"Yes." Ajay answered in a monosyllable. The entire drive was amazing, but Ajay was in a foul mood. A lovely trek, a sense of achievement at reaching 12,000 feet, the best '*darshan*' ever in a temple, the historical significance of the place, the rendezvous with the baba, the eagle sighting, all of it was spoilt by this one phone call.

Thirty minutes later, they reached the camp. Both Ajay and Atul silently covered the half a kilometre from the parking to the tents. After freshening up, they sat outside enjoying the cool breeze. Ajay was uncharacteristically silent.

"What's the matter?" Atul asked.

"Nothing, just leave me alone."

"Everything fine at home? Whose call was it that has affected your mood?"

"It was my Director."

"You should not let petty things from office spoil such a great day."

"*Baat hi kuch aisi hain, Atul.* I came away to escape from the office worries, and the one phone call that gets connected is from my Director."

"It's a sign."

"Now you shut up with that sign business. You are irritating me since afternoon."

Ajay's anger at his Director, burst out at Atul. Atul did not react and was calm.

"What did he say?"

"I have been offered, sorry given a job change. I am doing so well in Operations, suddenly they are uprooting me and asking me to take over HR once I return from my vacation."

"Good for you, right?"

"Good my foot! Firstly, I have no experience of HR. Secondly the HR department is currently in extremely bad shape. Even God cannot turn it around."

"Maybe God is sending you to turn it around"

"What do you mean?"

"Forget it Ajay, don't let your Director's call spoil this wonderful day. You have successfully climbed Tungnath, let's celebrate. After all water is a great drink, provided you have it with the right spirit. Get your spirits high with your sense of achievement." With this, they toasted with two bottles of mineral water. In 'Dev Bhoomi' which is an alcohol free zone, your spirits really need to be high.

"You are right. I shall solve this problem when I am back in Mumbai. The Abhimanyu story was fantastic right?"

"Yes I find it fascinating, the way Abhimanyu learnt how to enter the Chakravyuh. Also it is interesting that Subhadra fell asleep when Arjuna was talking about how to break the Chakravyuh and exit. This is exactly what happens when the audience is not interested in your story. Tell me how many times have you slept in boring corporate meetings?"

"Shut up." Ajay threw the empty mineral water bottle at Atul. Suddenly he started laughing and said,

"You know what, similar things happen in our corporate life. I am sure that in these town hall presentations by senior management, there are enough Subhadras who are not interested in what the senior management is saying and hence are asleep with their eyes wide awake."

Atul's linking of Subhadra to corporate life had lightened the mood.

"Do you think Abhimanyu was forced to enter the Chakravyuh?"

"I don't think so Atul. I think he showed exceptional leadership qualities."

"See Ajay, you are the corporate guy. I am just a guy who lives on water."

Ajay laughed. It was a brilliant pun by Atul as he was a teetotaller and earned his living from a water sport like surfing.

"Tell me Ajay, what do you think are his leadership qualities?"

"If you remember the story, that was a time when Abhimanyu's father Arjuna was engaged in a different part of the battlefield. The Kaurava army was creating havoc. It was a crisis situation. Somebody had to step up and take charge."

"Do you think it was foolish of him to enter the Chakravyuh?" Atul asked Ajay.

"Atul, are you mad? In a crisis situation, you do not deliberate. You act. Execution and Speed is the key."

"Even if you don't have enough knowledge? Tell me, would you have taken the same decision Ajay?"

"No doubt about that Atul. That is what leadership is. Let's do a proper risk assessment of the situation. If Abhimanyu had not acted then, his team and he would anyway have been destroyed. They were outnumbered and losing fast. They had only one chance, a slim chance of winning if they managed to break the Chakravyuh. They had to take that risk. Actually if you ask me it was a no brainer."

"So what leadership qualities did Abhimanyu display?"

"Proper Risk Assessment, Quick Decision Making, Leading by Example, Taking Charge and Trust in his people. We hear similar stories from the Indian Army."

"If I know you well, Ajay, I think the Baba was right."

"What?"

"He said you are Abhimanyu. I have known you for nearly 25 years now. I think you display all the qualities that Abhimanyu did." Ajay and Atul had met on Day 1 of college. Thus began a friendship, which was close to completing 25 years.

"Thanks for the compliment Atul. My day just keeps on getting better."

"I have heard that with growing age, cowardice sets in. Is that happening to you?"

"What do you mean Atul?"

"Why are you so disgusted about your transfer?"

"I just don't want to work in HR"

"Is it that you don't want to work in HR, or are you afraid of failure?"

"Watch what you are saying Atul." Fifteen years of corporate life, develops an ego. If anybody else had said this to Ajay, he would have reacted more violently. Childhood friends are the only ones who can get away with such statements.

"What are you unhappy about Ajay? Is it the fact that you are being uprooted from Operations, or that you are being moved to HR?"

"Both."

"I will tell you what is on your mind. You know Operations like the back of your hand. You are an expert at it, and you will succeed. HR is completely new to you. You are being moved out of your comfort zone."

"Maybe you are right."

"Why are they sending you, an Operations guy to HR and not a professional HR person?"

"I have no clue."

"In the past have you seen an Operations guy join HR?"

"No."

"Does your Director hate you?"

"Actually no, I am one of his trusted lieutenants."

"Are you sure?"

"Of course. Even the Board has great faith in me."

"Then here is the answer. Till now, HR has been handled by HR professionals, who have succeeded in running it to the ground. As you said HR is already at rock bottom. You have had great success in Operations, you are respected and maybe you are considered the turnaround man. You can't do any more damage. HR's job is to create a good working environment. Once you reach the bottom, the only way is up."

"Yes, but this is not what I want to do. It is a diversion from my career path."

"The more I think of this, the more I have started believing in the Baba."

"What are you saying Atul?"

"Ajay, the Baba said two things. He said that you are Abhimanyu. I believe him because I know your leadership qualities."

"Thank you for the compliment Atul, but you still have to pay for your share of the trip."

"What kind of a friend are you, you will take money from a friend?"

"Of course! All friends are rascals!"

"The second thing that the baba mentioned is that you are going to have an Abhimanyu experience."

"Which means I am going to be sacrificed!! Cheers to that." Ajay retorted sarcastically.

"Ajay you still don't get it. We agreed that Abhimanyu was not forced to enter the Chakravyuh. He displayed great leadership qualities. Actually your situation is worse than Abhimanyu. You are being thrown into a situation which you don't like, which you have no experience of and you don't want to do. You don't even know how to enter the Chakravyuh, leave alone break it from inside. Why do you think the Board and Director are putting you into this situation without your consent?"

"Food is ready sir." The cook came and called them for dinner. Even though there was a dining area, they preferred to have dinner in the kitchen. The kitchen was a small hut where firewood was used to cook the food.

Ajay and Atul had no intention of eating in the biting cold outside. Also, by the time the hot *roti* would come to the table, it would get cold. They preferred to sit by the warmth of the fire, eating hot *rotis,* their eyes watering from the firewood smoke.

"You didn't answer my question Ajay."

"Which question?"

"Why do you think the Board and the Director are putting you into this situation without your consent?"

"I don't know. Let me think. I am from Operations, which means I understand where HR is going wrong. I know exactly what should not be done. I will be working in HR in a practical manner, not bringing fancy theories to the drawing board. I don't think I can do any worse than what HR is currently doing. You know what, the Board actually has faith in me."

"Very well said Ajay. Abhimanyu, knew the consequence of his actions. He knew that it could be a matter of life and death. As a warrior, a Kshatriya he was true to his Dharma (Call of Duty). What is your Dharma? Is it towards yourself and what you want to do, or is it towards your organisation?"

"Interesting question Atul, very difficult to answer. My Dharma is towards myself, my family as well as the organisation. And honestly don't ask me to prioritise or rank them in order. It is extremely difficult."

"I know what you are saying. Like Abhimanyu, you are entering a Chakravyuh with the responsibility to break the deadlock from within. There is one big difference. You are not being sent on a suicide mission, you are being sent to clear the mess. The chances are that you may fail, however I don't think you will die."

"That's reassuring Atul. Thanks. But I am still not convinced."

"Look, I think you are disgusted about the fact that you are being moved from an area which is your comfort zone, to an area which is completely unknown. And if the situation in HR is as bad as you are mentioning, you are afraid that you may not succeed; maybe you may not get the level of success that you are used to."

Ajay did not reply. He was internalising Atul's words, while chewing on a hot roti. Atul realised that and allowed Ajay to finish his roti and thoughts.

After a few moments, Atul punctuated the silence with "What if you succeed, Ajay?"

"The chances are slim." Ajay replied immediately.

"Ajay, you are so hell-bent on not joining HR that you are not even willing to think of success. For a moment, think, what will happen if you succeed?"

"I don't know. You tell me Mr. Know it All." Ajay was getting irritated by this conversation.

"You are in such a negative frame of mind right now that you don't want to look at the positives. In case you succeed, you will be a hero."

"Heroes look good only in movies. Let me be a mortal." Ajay quipped. His irritation had clouded his willingness to think.

"If you succeed, will you be next in line to succeed your CEO?" Unfortunately, Atul's sentence co-incided with Ajay's gargling. The impact was that water entered his nostrils from the mouth. He spluttered and was in discomfort for a few minutes. This discomfort gave him time to think of what Atul had said.

"I seriously didn't think of that."

"Now look at the coincidences. You have visited the highest Shiva temple in the world. You have meditated at the place where Lord Vishnu got his Sudarshan Chakra. Lord Vishnu's vehicle, the Eagle, came and gave you a beautiful sight of his flight. I say he blessed you. The only call you receive in an area where there is no mobile connectivity, is from your Director. You have been blessed and are destined to succeed."

Ajay suddenly remembered the baba's parting words.

"Mera ashirwaad hain, tum jaroor chakravyuh todke baahar aaoge." (I bless you that you will break through the chakravyuh and be successful.)

He had paid no attention to the significance of those words and just took them as blessings. As he pondered the events of the day, he realised that he had just been mentored by his friend who had never worked in a company. The force was with him.

———— ～ ————

YUDHISHTHIR'S DILEMMA

"Increase the revenue by 10% and decrease the direct cost by 10%. This will ensure that the project looks viable. We present this proposal to Pooja on Monday morning. Given that you have worked so hard on this, it will be your show. This needs to go through." Deven gave these instructions and left for the day.

It was 10 at night and Megha was tired. She saved the presentation and calculations on her laptop and went home. Monday would be a big day in her life. It was her first big proposal and she was both tense and excited. If the proposal went through, it would put her company on a massive growth track. Deven and Megha had worked on this proposal for nearly two months.

Megha was a Chartered Accountant and had been working with Jamero which had begun as a start-up in the ecommerce space. It was her first job, and shunning conventional wisdom, she had joined Jamero. The pay was not great, but there were Employee Stock Option Plans (ESOPs) attached.

Jamero, which was the brainchild of Pooja, developed an application (app) which would help people track various details around their health. The app had become popular; the firm had got venture capital funding and grown. Deven, the CFO of Jamero, was the key person dealing with investors, and Megha was his go to person. Every financial proposal, projections etc. were prepared by Megha. Eventually Pooja sold the concept, app and brand name and made a killing.

With the money Pooja made, she was looking at investing in new ventures and needed Deven's guidance. She liked Megha's hard work and integrity and realised that here was an asset she should not let go of. On the way out of Jamero, she asked both of them to join her in the investment office.

Actually, the exit idea came from Deven. With 20 years of experience, he was extremely talented and had huge contacts and was the brain behind Pooja's venture. While the ecommerce space was growing, he was convinced it was getting too crowded. It was the time, where everybody with even a semblance of an idea was getting venture capital and private equity funding. It reminded him of the dotcom boom. Deven felt that in three years, every venture capitalist, private equity firm etc. would be heading for an exit and was not sure that exit would be possible. None of the firms in the ecommerce space looked like having a revenue model and were burning cash daily. He convinced Pooja to exit and get into a business venture which had a proper revenue model, realistic cash flows and in turn, real profits.

Both Deven and Megha had been rewarded with stock options during their stint at Jamero and both had cashed out. Megha had done so reluctantly, as she believed that the value will grow over time. It was a contrarian call, but she could not refute Deven's strong logic and decided to trust her senior. The new buyers of Jamero had wanted her to stay back, but the opportunity to continue working with Deven was too good to pass. Also with encashing of the stock options, she was financially secure. She was young and could afford to take a risk.

With money in the bag, she decided to indulge herself and quickly found herself on a flight to visit her cousin in California. On a trip to Universal Studios, an idea stuck her. Why can't we have multiple theme parks across the country in India? She actually visited Universal Studios again, this time to look at the systems, architecture and landscaping of the rides, ticketing system etc. She was hell bent on talking about this to Pooja and Deven.

Both of them were excited and Pooja had given them two months to come up with a project proposal. Megha had researched this extensively for two months and now it was her baby.

Megha wanted to go through the project proposal in close detail over the weekend. On Saturday morning, she received a call from Sameer, her boyfriend, who wanted to meet her for lunch. Megha flatly refused saying that she had to work on her project proposal.

Close friends go beyond what is said and can understand feelings which are not expressed. Even in the age of WhatsApp, they understand the emotions behind the words. The human heart has some innate capabilities, which even science can't explain. Come to think of it, today we have WhatsApp, fifty years ago there were letters. The art of communication with written words exists from centuries. Is it coming back with WhatsApp? Is this what is called the circle of life?

Sameer was not new to such refusals and could take them in his stride. Megha was fiercely independent, and in love with Sameer, but the entire relationship was on her terms. However this day's conversation was different. Megha was firm in her refusal to join him for lunch but Sameer could sense something different in her voice. Intuitively, it seemed that she was screaming out wanting to meet him. Sameer decided to respect her choice of not meeting him for lunch but decided to meet her later on in the day.

He landed up at her house at five in the evening. Megha was startled, but secretly happy. Generally, after a nap people are fresh, however Megha was a mess and looked as if a truck had run over her. Sameer sensed that her physical appearance was the result of her mental state. Ten minutes later, Megha came out looking slightly better.

"What are you doing here Sameer?"

"*Tere pyaar mein judai ka gham saha nahin gaya*" (I could not bear to be away from you)

"Abe tera filmy dialogue band kar. I told you, I have work." (Stop being romantic, I told you I have work)

Now the human ego is complicated. Even though Megha was happy that Sameer had come, she would not admit it.

"I thought, if not lunch, at least let me have a cup of coffee with you. See Megha, our schedules don't allow us to meet during weekdays. And if I don't meet you over the weekend also, how will I survive the next week? *Kahin tere judaai mein mar nahin jau."* (I hope I don't die longing for you)

Megha laughed and the tension broke. *"Tu filmy ka filmy hi rahega. Bol kya chal rahaa hain."* (Stop your cheesy dialogues. Tell me how are things.)

"I am doing fine Megha, enjoying life. Every day of the week I look forward to meeting you over the weekend. As of now life is beautiful. You tell me, what's the tension in your life?"

"How do you know I am stressed Sameer?"

"Megha, I have known you for five years, I can feel your stress even from your WhatsApp messages. I realised something was wrong during our chat when you refused to meet me."

"Sameer, tum Antaryami ho!" (Sameer you have occult powers!!)

"Woh to main hoon. Bol teri pareshani kya hain bachcha... Meri baahon mein aao, saari pareshani khatam ho jayegi!!"

(Definitely I have occult powers. Tell me what's troubling you child. Come in my arms and all your troubles will go away.)

"Sameer, you are wasting your time in corporate. You have a career as a godman... You have even started talking in a lecherous manner."

"Beta... mere badan se lipat jaogi, to meri shakti tumhare badan mein aa jayegi aur teri uljhan sulajh jaayegi" (Child, hold me tight, let me transfer the warmth from my body to yours and all your problems will go away.)

Megha flung the newspaper at Sameer and both started laughing.

"Tell me the problem."

"You know the theme park project I am working on? I have to present it to Pooja on Monday."

"Fantastic! Monday is your big day and I am sure you will do well. Pooja will be floored and agree to fund the project. How come you are scared of the presentation?"

"I am never afraid of any presentations. It's just that...."

And suddenly, just like that, Megha broke down. The flood of emotions that had been piled up since the last few days burst forth in front of Sameer's genuine concern.

One thing men can't handle, is a crying woman. They just don't know how to react. In Megha's house, Sameer couldn't even take her in his arms and comfort her.

He started looking at the ceiling, out of the window, towards the dark switched off TV, trying to conjure non-existent images... He was extremely uncomfortable. He was thinking what happened, what did he say? He went through the conversation of the last few minutes, in his mind. Did his sudden appearance upset Megha? Was his lecherous godman act offensive? Suddenly Megha's mom came out. Sameer felt like a deer caught in the headlights. Though Megha's parents knew of Sameer, that he was their prospective son-in-law and also approved of him, he was embarrassed. No man can handle such a situation, where a girl is crying and her parents come in.

However Megha's mom knew both Sameer and Megha very well. She smiled at him, gave him a glass of water and gestured to him to offer it to Megha. Then, she went back into her room. Sameer offered the water to Megha, who drank it and excused herself.

The room felt awfully silent after Megha walked out, so Sameer switched on the TV. It was a music channel and was airing the promotion of *"Ek Paheli Leela"*, with Sunny Leone dancing.

"Sameer!!!"

"At least don't watch Sunny Leone in my house and in my presence."

Shit!! This day was going from bad to worse. Sameer thought that he would have been better off watching the IPL match at home over beer and chips. He had to salvage the situation.

"You just told me about a new career, I was researching for that."

"What?" Megha just did not understand.

"You told me I should become a lecherous godman, I am researching that"

A wooden coaster missed Sameer's face by a few inches. Tension diffused.

"Tell me Megha, is there a problem with your project?"

"Let me tell you the whole story. You know I got this idea about a theme park, when I visited the US. I talked about it to Pooja and Deven, and both of them were excited about it. Deven and I have been working on this over the last two months. We have been looking at various theme parks, identifying what rides to have, talking to equipment suppliers etc. You remember a month ago, when we went to Imagica? I was mixing business with pleasure. I was looking at the architecture, identifying its flaws, looking at the rides which are in demand etc. Over the last two months, we have been talking to landscape architects, other architects, getting the costing in etc. But, when we look at the projections, it looks like the project may not make money."

"So then Megha, are you disappointed, that your pet project, where you have put in your heart and soul may not see the light of day?"

"No it is not that. It is the conversations that I have been having with Deven, that are creating problems. We have been going through the financial projections over the last two weeks. At the first cut, it was clear that this was a loss making project. Over the last two weeks, we have been trying to cut the jigsaw to fit it. We have increased the projected revenues and tweaked the costs, just to make it look profitable. And during all of this, it is Deven who is pushing me to make the changes. He says that in future years, we will show increased ticket prices, which will lead to higher revenues, which will make the project feasible. On the other hand, he has been cunning enough to keep costs in check, which makes it look profitable. Last night, before leaving, he asks me to increase revenues by 10% and reduce costs by 10% which makes the project look viable. Tell me, how do I present a project which I don't believe in?"

"Hmmm. Interesting problem. You want to tell the truth and don't know what to do, reminds me of Yudhishthir. What do you think of him Megha?"

"I don't know any Yudhishthir."

"The Pandava king from the Mahabharata."

"The one who wagered his wife? Sameer, what are your intentions? A few minutes ago you were talking like a lecherous godman, and now about a guy who wagers his wife? I got to think, whether I should marry you or not!"

It was Megha's turn to indulge in some playful banter.

"Shut up Megha. Do you know what Yudhishtir was famous for?"

"Other than wagering his wife, what?'

"He was supposed to be honest... he would never tell a lie."

"So you want me to tell Pooja the truth? Wow, Sameer you have just lifted a load off my chest."

"There are layers to Yudhishthir. I mentioned, he was supposed to be honest."

"Are you hinting at something? Did he actually tell a lie?"

"Let me tell you a story. During the Mahabharata war, Dronacharya was leading the Kaurava army. The Kaurava princes were always suspicious of Dronacharya, as Arjuna was his favourite student. His ability to fight his favourite student was questioned. However people of those times were true to their dharma, their duty. He led the Kauravas with great vigour and it was feared that the Pandavas would be defeated. The Pandavas knew that Dronacharya had to be taken out of the equation. Defeating him in combat was difficult. A situation had to be created where he would lay down his arms himself. His weak point was his son Ashwatthama.

The Pandavas hatched a plot. They killed an elephant named Ashwatthama and floated a rumour that Ashwatthama was killed in battle. This would kill Dronacharya's spirit and he would lay down his arms. When Dronacharya heard the rumour, he didn't believe it. He saw through the ruse. However the rumour became stronger by the minute. One part of his mind, was wondering, what if it is actually true? He decided to confront Yudhishthir who was known for telling the truth."

Here Sameer stopped his narration to ask Megha a question.

"Megha, is your situation similar to Yudhishthir's?"

"You are right Sameer. My heart and soul is in the project, and the profitability is suspect. I have reworked the numbers, but the dilemma is, what do I tell Pooja on Monday morning? Do I tell her the truth, or sell her the profitable projections? On the one hand, I don't want to tell a lie, on the other I want the project to go through. Sameer, you are amazing. You are really wasting your time. You have potential as a godman. If you drop the lecherous part, I will get married to you!"

"Thanks for the compliment Megha. But let's analyse the situation in greater detail. There are two issues here. If you tell the truth, your pet project, your baby will be aborted. I know how difficult it is. First let us analyse whether you need to tell the truth or the half-truth."

"In case you are reporting a number to the regulators, you need to tell the truth. If you don't do that you are committing an offence. So in that case, whatever be the repercussions, you have to tell the truth, because that is the right thing to do. Not everybody does that and I respect your ethics Megha."

"However this situation is different. What you are showcasing on Monday, is projections. These are projections around cost, revenue, profits. There are assumptions around what you can charge customers, the number of customers that will come in etc. These projections and assumptions may or may not come true. Hence what you are projecting is just an estimate. What difference does it make if you listen to Deven? Your projections can go wrong, but your pet project will go through!"

"Are you mad Sameer? You are asking me to mask my lies under assumptions and projections? I thought you were honest Sameer, I am discovering a new side to you." Now Megha was really angry.

Sameer sensed her anger. "Ok let's get back to Yudhishthir. What do you think he did when Dronacharya confronted him? Remember he knew that it was Ashwatthama the elephant and not Dronacharya's son, who was killed in battle."

"I don't know."

"What would you have done? Would you have told the truth? Before answering, think of the consequences. By telling the truth, Yudhishthir could have actually helped decimate the Pandavas and they could have lost their war and maybe even their lives."

"Difficult situation Sameer. I really don't know. The more I think, the more I feel that it is similar to my situation, however the consequences aren't that dire. What did Yudhishthir do?"

"When Dronacharya confronted Yudhishthir, he said Ashwatthama has been killed in battle. In a small voice, under his breath, he said, 'the elephant'."

"In reality, he said 'Ashwatthama, *the elephant (under his breath),* has been killed in battle. So technically, he didn't lie, but Dronacharya thought it was his son who was killed and laid down his arms."

"Wow this is amazing. Now I get what you say. I am wondering whether I should do a Yudhishthir."

"Not so fast Megha. Two actions of Yudhishthir have damaged his reputation. One, the fact that he wagered his brothers and wife. Second, the 'part truth / untruth' that he uttered. Remember any action that you take, will hurt your reputation."

Now Megha was thinking fast. She understood what Sameer was saying. She understood the deep meaning of the story. She would do a Yudhishthir on Monday and leave the decision to Pooja. She would present multiple scenarios without masking the truth. She would emphasize on the numbers she believed in, and leave it to Pooja to take a decision. It was good that Deven had given her the freedom. She had to take her own decision in a way where it would not hurt Deven, keep her reputation intact, and present a correct picture to Pooja.

"Thanks Sameer, you have cleared my entire dilemma. Now I am relaxed. Let's go and watch a movie. *Kaunsa picture jayenge?*" (Which movie do you want to watch?)

"Ek Paheli Leela."

This time the coaster found its target!!!

———⌇———

KUNTI & KARNA

"So gentlemen and ladies, thank you all for coming today to this important meeting. I have an announcement to make. Rajeev, who has headed sales for the last ten years, has decided to move on. He intends to spend time pursuing his passions and we respect his decision. He will be with us for the next one year and continue to head sales. Nine months from now we will meet to announce who will be the next head of sales. It will definitely be one of you. The lucky person will take over nine months from now, and Rajeev will guide this person for three months after that. All the best to all of you!" With this the Managing Director dismissed the meeting. Everybody rushed to congratulate Rajeev and ask him about his future plans. At the back of everybody's mind there was one question – who would be the successor?

Even though there were six sales heads in the room, it was clearly a two horse race. Historically, the head of sales always came from either the lighting products division or the consumer products division. Combined together, the two divisions contributed to more than 60% of sales and more than 40% of profits. Simeran was the head of the consumer products division which for five years in a row had edged out the lighting products division, albeit by a small margin in terms of growth. Every year, the consumer products division had grown by more than 25%. It had expanded into new territories and the products had huge brand recall. Simeran had joined the firm as a management trainee straight from B-School and within seven years had grown to head the consumer products division. Her growth in the organisation was extremely fast and nobody disputed that. She was young, had age on her side and was tipped to be Managing Director one day.

Shardul, true to his name was a tiger and was heading the lighting products division for the last five years. Ironically, Simeran had worked under his leadership in the consumer products division and together they had carried it to great heights. Five years ago, he had handed over the consumer products division to Simeran and moved to the lighting products division. Both were now peers and fierce competitors and also great friends. As a matter of fact Shardul was instrumental in Simeran's last two promotions. Shardul's handing over of the consumer products division, resulted in Simeran's promotion and elevated her to a seat next to Shardul. Shardul was happy that Simeran was beating Shardul's division marginally over the last five years. After all, every guru is happy when the ward outperforms the master.

Shardul was actually eight years older than Simeran and had grown through the organisation. He had all round experience of various divisions and was the hot favourite to replace Rajeev. However it was not a foregone conclusion. Simeran was an extremely strong contender. The race was actually too close to call.

Word spread around the firm about Rajeev's move and the topic of discussion on every table was Simeran vs. Shardul. While Simeran and Shardul did not have any open rivalry, the organisation was getting divided into two camps.

******

Divya's sleep was disturbed by the cell phone ringing. Five missed calls from Prashant. She panicked and called him back.

"Prashant, you okay?"

"Absolutely fine dear, I need your help."

"Where are you?" Divya feared the worst.

"At home, but I need your help."

"What's the problem Prashant?"

"Everything's fine but I need to talk to you."

When she heard this, Divya lost it. Two thirty in the morning was not the time to talk. Especially not for two grown up people who were way beyond the courting stage. They were engaged and scheduled to get married in three months.

"Are you drunk Prashant?"

"I am in my senses but I've lost my mind." Prashant mumbled.

"Listen Prashant, I am switching off my phone. Let's meet tomorrow evening and talk about whatever you want. But right now let's go to sleep."

Divya was an Associate in the Compliance team of a leading financial services company. She was extremely organised, well planned and meticulous. She hated these middle of the night conversations.

Next evening, she arrived at Cafe Di Bella at Mahim in an extremely angry mood. She had decided to give Prashant a piece of her mind. She reached there to find that Prashant had not yet arrived. Criminal, one never makes a lady wait. Divya's anger was growing by the minute. In a few minutes a taxi stopped and Prashant stepped out. He had brought a huge bunch of roses. Roses can melt every woman's temper and Divya was no exception. When they sat down at the table, Prashant opened his bag and plucked out a box of Dark Chocolate, Divya's favourite.

"I am extremely sorry Divya about those late night calls. Actually, I was drunk and the situation screamed that I need to speak to someone."

By now Divya's temper had completely melted and she was in a mood to talk. She was also concerned about Prashant's behaviour the previous night. She had known him for seven years now, and he was not one who called his girlfriend in a drunken state of mind, in the middle of the night. Something must be really bothering him.

"What's the matter Prashant?"

"Well, yesterday I went out for drinks with Shardul!"

"No!!"

"Yes I did. And guess what, he made me an offer. He wants me to join his team."

"What? And why so?"

"You are aware that Rajeev, the head of sales is leaving."

"Yes. So what?"

"Shardul believes that he will be the next head of sales."

"Is that right Prashant?"

"Well, I don't know. It is a very close call and one really can't say."

"So what does Shardul want?"

"Shardul was very candid. He says that the only thing that can come between him and his elevation is the fact that he does not have a ready successor. He wants me to join his team and start the handover, so that when the time comes, he is ready to be relieved from his current job."

"Fantastic Prashant, so what's your problem?"

"Well, I respect Shardul, but all along I have worked with Simeran. She is also projecting me as her successor. I need to decide whether I want to head the consumer products division or the lighting division. What do I do Divya?"

"All along you have worked in the consumer products division, now suddenly you are being put in the lighting division, will you be able to handle it?"

"That's exactly the question I asked Shardul. He cites his example and says that if he can do it, so can I."

Prashant had joined the consumer products division after his MBA. He was two batches junior to Simeran and had been handpicked by her during their campus placements. He and Simeran were a team. When Shardul headed consumer products division, Prashant was the ground level executor for every strategy conceived by Simeran and Shardul. The three of them were instrumental in taking consumer products to where it was. Subsequently once Shardul moved out, he became Simeran's right hand. In case Simeran were to be elevated to head of sales, Prashant was the hot favourite to take her position as head of consumer products division.

"The decision is easy Prashant. If you are to become head of sales in future, you need experience across multiple divisions. You have experience in consumer products and now lighting is falling in your lap."

Suddenly Divya's phone beeped. It was a message. Normally Divya would open the messages once a day and never in the company of Prashant. For some unknown reason she opened it. It was from Sony TV, a promotional quiz based on their new daily serial, 'Karna'. Unlike her regular behaviour Divya decided to answer the quiz.

"Prashant, who was Karna's biological mother, Radha, Kunti or Madri? Radha right?"

"What?" Prashant could not believe his ears. Here he was talking about his career move, which was crucial to him and Divya was interested in Karna's biological roots. That is the difference between men and women. Men think about one topic at a time, while women are capable of processing information about multiple topics at the same time. Which is why sometimes, no always, men don't understand women.

"Karna is not a Pandava, so obviously his mother cannot be Kunti or Madri, so she should be Radha correct?"

Prashant gave up. After all, she was his fiancée and he decided he better get used to this kind of deviations which would be regular after their marriage.

"Incorrect Divya, Karna was Kunti's son, abandoned by her at birth. He was brought up by a charioteer Adhirath and his wife Radha."

"Did Karna know that while he was fighting the war?"

"Yes he did, Divya. Krishna had told him the story of his birth. The day Karna was to take over the leadership of the Kaurava army, Kunti also told him the truth about his birth. She told him that she had abandoned him as a child, as she was an unwed mother when he was born. She also requested him to join the Pandavas."

"So you mean to say, Kunti went to Karna to recruit him to fight from the Pandavas side?"

"Yes."

"Very interesting. How did Karna react?"

"Karna refused to join the Pandavas."

"Tell me, how did she come to know that Karna was her abandoned son?"

"Karna was the son of Surya the son god. He was born with kavacha-kundala, a protective armour and a set of earrings. Karna gate-crashed the graduation ceremony of Kaurava and Pandava princes, that is when Kunti saw him with the kavacha-kundala and recognised her son."

"What?" Divya looked up startled. She stared into space for a few minutes. Prashant started to say something, but Divya silenced him with a wave of her hand. Prashant had seen Divya in these moods before. It was as if Divya had seen a ghost. Or, as if she had stumbled upon some big secret which was right in front of her but she had been blind to it before. He knew that after a few minutes she would explain the situation to him. He looked around here and there blankly while waiting for her to speak again.

"Prashant, I need another coffee." There was a definite seriousness to Divya's voice. It was a clear signal that she had figured out the mystery and she would slowly explain it.

"Why do you think Karna refused to join the Pandavas?"

"He was loyal towards Duryodhana."

"Of course he was loyal towards Duryodhana. What else?"

"What else Divya?"

"I think loyalty is a big reason but not the only reason for Karna's refusal. I think he saw through Kunti's plan."

"What are you talking about Divya?"

"The game of dice was played at least a few years after the graduation ceremony?"

"Yes. What are you hinting at Divya?"

"Shut up and keep on answering my questions. Once the Pandavas lost in the game of dice, what was the punishment?"

"They were subject to twelve years of *vanvaas*, living in the forest and one year of *agyatvaas*, where they were to live incognito."

"So on a conservative calculation, there would be at least one decade if not more between the time Kunti recognised Karna was her son, and disclosing the truth to him?"

"Elementary my dear Watson. I know you are a fan of Sherlock Holmes. And your mathematics is also good, what are you trying to prove?"

"Do you think Kunti approached Karna more than ten years, I repeat years, not days after she recognised him as a son, because she loved him? What was the reason for her motherhood to suddenly come to the fore after decades?"

"What reason, Divya, she did not want that her own children should fight on both sides of the war."

"Bullshit Prashant, if she had love for Karna, she would have accepted him much earlier."

Prashant knew Divya was on to something. But he was getting irritated. He had called her to discuss his career move and not Kunti's love or otherwise for her child.

"Divya, can we come back to my career?"

"My dear *bhole*, do you realise we are actually talking about your career?"

He still did not understand what Divya was hinting at. But he trusted her and decided to continue the discussion.

"Ok, so Kunti did not love Karna. What next?"

"Were both Kauravas and Pandavas evenly matched during the war, or were Pandavas fiercely superior?"

"Actually, it was a very close contest, if you keep the result aside. Warriors like Bhishma and Dronacharya on the Kaurava side, made it an extremely close fight."

"What about Karna, was he one of the lead warriors for the Kauravas?"

"Yes, as a matter of fact, he was the only one capable of vanquishing Arjuna. Actually, after Bhishma and Dronacharya he was the third person to be appointed as the Kaurava general"

"What would have happened if Karna had accepted Kunti's proposal?"

"Duryodhana would have been extremely unhappy."

"Forget about Duryodhana. If Karna had accepted Kunti's proposal what would have happened to the balance of power pre-war?"

"It would have shifted decisively towards the Pandavas. With Karna and Arjuna fighting side by side, it would have been a winning combination. You know what, this combination reminds me of India- Pakistan and a conversation with my elder brother. In the eighties, both Indian and Pakistani cricket teams used to get beaten by Australia, England and the West Indies. My brother used to say, just imagine if partition had not happened, Imran Khan and Kapil Dev would be bowling together, Sunil Gavaskar, Dilip Vengsarkar, Zaheer Abbas and Javed Miandad would be batting and the team would be unbeatable."

"That was Kunti's plan. The Pandavas were actually afraid of Karna. Both Bhishma and Dronacharya had a soft corner towards the Pandavas which could be exploited. But Karna had no chink in his armour. He was capable of defeating the Pandavas. The master plan was to get Karna to defect, using an emotional plank."

"Divya that is an amazing deduction. All along Karna was ridiculed as a charioteer's son, and knew he was adopted and was looking for an identity. They could give that to him easily. What a masterplan."

"Unfortunately it did not work Prashant."

"It did Divya. Karna promised Kunti, that she would have five of her sons alive. He would kill only Arjuna in the battlefield. Krishna who was Arjuna's charioteer kept him away from Karna. Karna actually disarmed and defeated all the Pandavas in battle and spared their lives."

"Holy cow, I did not know this, so the master plan worked."

"The Pandavas ensured that all the leading generals from the Kauravas fought the war with one hand tied behind their back. Hats off to their strategy."

"Prashant..." Divya paused wondering whether to say the next few words. But then she decided she had to...

"Is Shardul doing a Kunti?"

Divya's question coincided with Prashant putting the coffee cup to his lips to take a sip. Prashant choked on his coffee...that is if one can choke on coffee! Like clumsy men, the coffee spurted out of his mouth and was all over the table and on Divya's face. Divya just smiled, got up and went to the washroom to clean herself. While the waiter was cleaning the mess on the table, the impact of Divya's words was sinking in.

Once Divya was back, she leaned back on the sofa and looked at Prashant with an inquisitive smile.

"What?"

"Answer my question Prashant, Is Shardul doing a Kunti?"

"Preposterous Divya. Shardul is not that type of person. He was instrumental in ensuring Simeran was promoted. He was the one who handed the consumer products division to Simeran."

He remembered the multiple discussions he, Shardul and Simeran used to have. They used to brainstorm and fight to reach a conclusion. There were multiple times when he had to play referee between Shardul and Simeran. Simeran had a huge respect for Shardul and had mentioned it to Prashant that they were fortunate to be working with him.

"Let's for a moment forget all that you just said. Just answer my questions."

"You are being groomed to be the head of the consumer products division?"

"Yes."

"If you move over to Shardul's team, is there anybody ready to fill your shoes?"

"Yes, Manoj is ready...."

Manoj was part of Prashant's team. Prashant had already delegated a lot of his work to Manoj and had begun to increasingly rely on him.

"Manoj might be ready to take over your role, but is he ready to take over from Simeran in case she is promoted as head of sales?

"No, Manoj is a few light years behind."

"Exactly, so if you move over to Shardul's team, who do you think, will be the next head of sales?"

Now it was Prashant's turn to see the ghost.

"Elementary my dear Watson." Exclaimed Divya and smilingly sipped on her coffee

"But Shardul can never do that, he has always been so supportive of Simeran."

Prashant recollected that Shardul would mention quite a few times, that one day he would end up reporting to Simeran, and Simeran would dismiss that thought. Was this mentioned in jest or was it Shardul's real fear?

"Insecurity my dear friend, insecurity. When Simeran was promoted and handed over the consumer products division, Rajeev wasn't going anywhere. Shardul was her senior and did not perceive any threat from her. By your own account, now it is an extremely close call. Do you think Shardul does not know this?"

"Point Divya."

"If Simeran becomes head of sales, will Shardul be comfortable reporting to her? Shardul is extremely smart. By recruiting you, he is ensuring these uncomfortable situations don't arise."

"Wow! Great reading of the situation Divya. So should I say no to Shardul?"

"Well, you are in a win-win situation. Both Simeran and Shardul want you to step into their shoes."

"Great discussion Divya, really enjoyed it, but still don't know what to do."

"Well, Prashant, Shardul is really a tiger. He is using you to play corporate politics. When it comes to survival he seems to be a champion. He will cut Simeran's candidature without her even realising it. Trust me, I am sure he will be the next head of sales."

"Divya, I suddenly don't like this. I think I will tell this deduction of ours to Simeran."

"Hang on Prashant, let me tell you what I would do in this situation. But before that, let me ask you a few questions."

"Shoot."

"Shardul is a nice guy, but has a great survival instinct. Is Simeran politically naive or suave like Shardul?"

"I think Simeran is pretty naive."

"Ok, so here is what I would do. Given that all along you have worked with Simeran, it is time to work with Shardul. You will learn stuff from Shardul, which will be different than what you have or will learn from Simeran. You need to learn these political nuances and who better than Shardul to teach you? Today you are Simeran's junior, in nine months you will be sitting next to her. Remember, you are just two years her junior, which is not significant. If Simeran, being eight years junior to Shardul, can sit next to him, you definitely can sit next to Simeran."

"Definitely worth pondering."

"You know Prashant, Shardul inspires me. Five years later if Shardul decides to move out, who knows? You could get the opportunity! You now have to think as to what do you need to do to be eligible for the top job? Having experience across multiple product lines, definitely ticks a few boxes."

"But what about my loyalty to Simeran?"

"It's not a war Prashant. Your decision is not going to destroy lives. You said that Simeran looks up to Shardul, and Shardul himself has been instrumental in Simeran's fast growth. There is no animosity between Simeran and Shardul. Even though you guys say it is close, I think Shardul will tip the scales. Simeran will be disappointed but will not mind Shardul's elevation much. She will actually be happy for him. I am sure the management understands this. You only have to ensure you don't destroy any relationships."

"How do I do this?"

"You dumbo Prashant, enrol Shardul to bat for you. Ask him to speak to Simeran. Remember he needs you more than you need him today."

Prashant was amazed at Divya's understanding and interpretation of the situation. He was sure that at some point of time, her career would outgrow his!

———◦∼◦———

ABOUT THE AUTHOR

Meghdoot Karnik is an accountant by qualification and a trainer by profession with twenty years experience spread over corporate and educational institutions. A teacher at heart, and an avid golfer, he is a voracious reader with specific interests in sports and mythology. He is currently a management consultant and a corporate trainer.

He blogs under the name of Dronacharya. This is his first book.

www.meghdootkarnik.com

meghdootkarnik.blogspot.in

dronacharya@meghdootkarnik.com

www.facebook.com/dronacharya8workplace

@Meghdootk

www.ingramcontent.com/pod-product-compliance
Lightning Source LLC
Chambersburg PA
CBHW022039190326
41520CB00008B/648